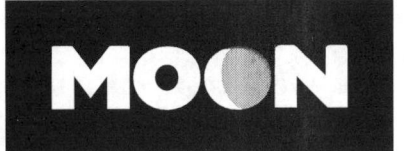

MOON SPOTLIGHT



# NEWPORT

MICHAEL BLANDING & ALEXANDRA HALL

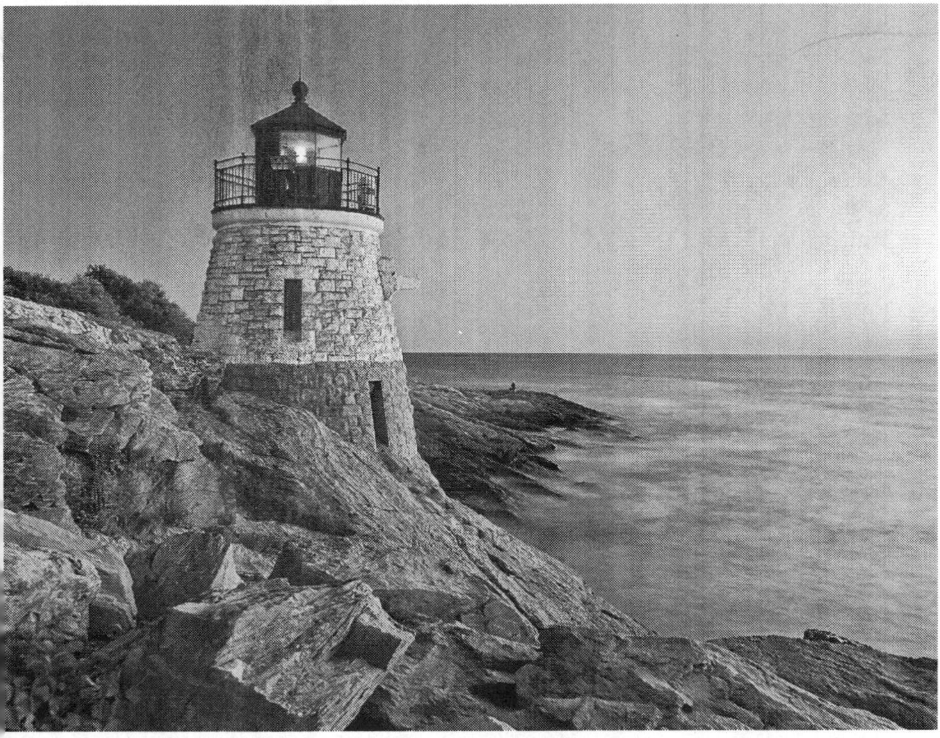

# Contents

## Newport ...4
History ...5
Planning Your Time ...10

## Sights ...10
Downtown and the Harbor ...10
The Point District ...16
Broadway ...17
Ocean Drive ...17
Rough Point ...18
Bellevue Avenue ...19
Newport's Mansions ...23
Cliff Walk ...29
Middletown ...31
Portsmouth ...34
Jamestown ...35

## Entertainment and Events ...35
Arts and Culture ...35
Nightlife ...35
Festivals and Events ...36

## Shopping ...39
Shopping Districts ...39
Arts and Crafts ...40
Antiques, Gifts, and Home Furnishings ...41
Pick-Your-Own Farms ...41

## Sports and Recreation ...41
First, Second, and Third Beaches ...41
Other Beaches ...43
Bicycling ...43
Boating ...43
Fishing ...44
Gaming ...44
Golf ...44
Ice-Skating ...44
Polo ...45
Scuba Diving ...45
Tennis ...45

## Accommodations ...45

## Food ...54

## Information and Services ...63
Visitor Information ...63
Media ...63

## Getting There and Around ...64
Buses ...64
Driving and Parking ...64
Taxis ...64
Ferry Service ...65
Tours ...65

# NEWPORT

© LEIGHTON OCONNOR/123RF.COM

# NEWPORT

But for historical happenstance, Newport might easily have become the largest city in New England. It's hard to imagine this elegant, sometimes almost quaint peninsula of colonial homes and lavish mansions instead studded with glass-and-steel skyscrapers, but Newport was headed in that direction until the Revolutionary War, and even for a time afterward. Originally one of the most successful ports in the New World, Newport saw its fortunes dashed by the war, in which most of its residents fled from the occupying British, and its star was quickly eclipsed by the thriving ports of Boston and New York.

Newport's resurgence began in the 19th century, when it became a favored destination for the Victorian moneyed class, who built enormous mansions on its cliffs, each more opulent than the last. Those mansions are still one of Newport's—and Rhode Island's—main draws for visitors, but the city has many other historical and recreational sites to recommend it as well.

Befitting its reputation as a yachting hub, Newport remains fairly preppy and conservative in its demeanor, though not its politics. This is a tolerant, socially progressive city with a relatively democratic (with a small *d*) edge. Sure, it's still scattered with seaside mansions once owned by eminent families with names like Duke and Astor, and certainly it still draws plenty of modern-day celebrities, CEOs, and astoundingly preppy families. But it also welcomes a salad of others: artists, college students, mansion gawkers, and bona fide sailors, all of whom congregate on Thames Street and

COURTESY OF PRESERVATION SOCIETY OF NEWPORT

# HIGHLIGHTS

LOOK FOR ◖ TO FIND RECOMMENDED SIGHTS, ACTIVITIES, DINING, AND LODGING.

◖ **Touro Synagogue:** The oldest Jewish house of worship in the United States dates to 1763 and serves a congregation that started in the 1650s (page 11).

◖ **The Point District:** Newport's most notable colonial neighborhood has enjoyed an astounding renaissance in recent years. Today it has the finest concentration of colonial architecture in New England (page 16).

◖ **Ocean Drive:** Arguably the most stunning shore drive on the East Coast, Ocean Drive reveals one gorgeous photo op after another (page 17).

◖ **Rough Point:** The former summer home of heiress Doris Duke, this late Victorian mansion on a rocky point overlooking the ocean has been left furnished almost exactly as when Duke lived in it. Guests are welcome to relax on the gracious grounds for as long as they'd like after their tour (page 18).

◖ **The Breakers:** Cornelius Vanderbilt's little summer cottage is simply the most stunning of all Newport's mansions – and that's saying a lot (page 26).

◖ **Cliff Walk:** You can enjoy a memorable 3.5-mile stroll along this fabled oceanfront path that fringes some of Newport's most expensive and famous mansions, including The Breakers and Rough Point. It's Newport's best free activity (page 29).

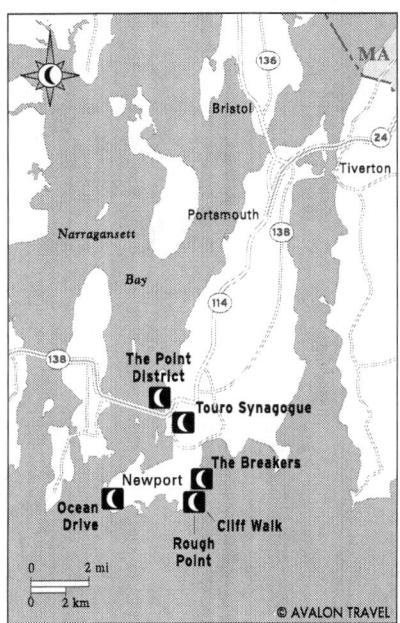

the waterfront to create an unparalleled people-watching experience.

Looking around this busy but small-scale city today, with its stunning parks and green spaces, its fine homes of all styles, and diversions that include sailing charters, romantic inns, and posh boutiques, it's easy to guess that most of the city's residents and visitors are happy that fate chose not to turn Newport into another Boston or even Providence. There are big cities up and down the Eastern Seaboard, but few places have the combined charms of Newport.

# HISTORY

Settled in 1639, Newport began as one of early Rhode Island's typically tolerant colonies, a haven for those disenchanted with the religious and political conformity and ultimately oppression in the Massachusetts colonies. With a strategic, sheltered harbor, however, it wasn't long before enterprising locals turned the young city into a corner of the infamous Triangle Trade with the West Indies and Africa. Much of Newport's early trading was slave-oriented—in fact, Newport surpassed even Charleston, South Carolina, during the early years in the number of slaves that passed through its port.

Rhode Island's ban of slavery in 1774 did little to slow Newport's merchants, who continued to trade in rum, molasses, indigo, and other wares. The blow to the city's economic clout, and also its colonist pride, came at the

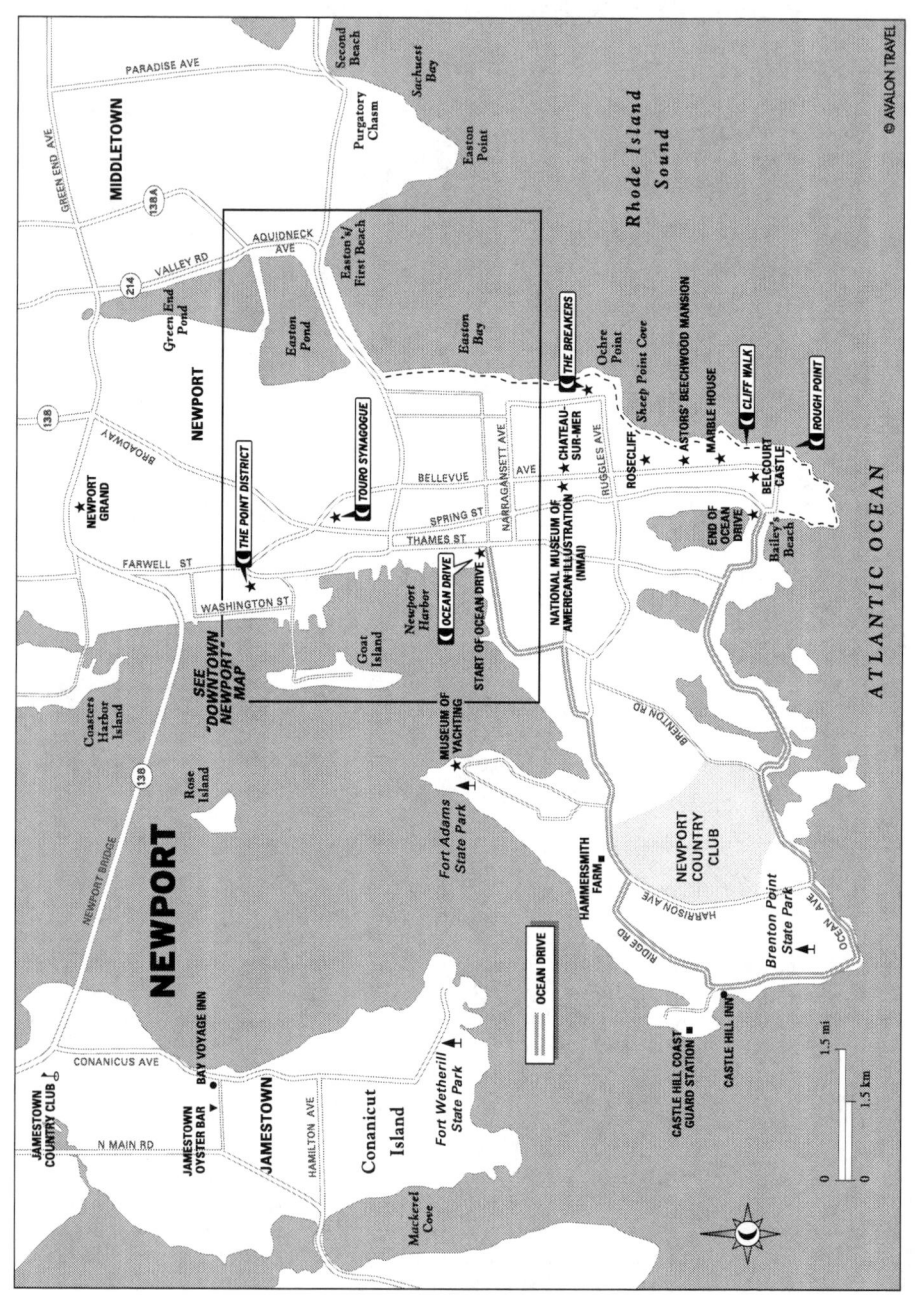

## NEWPORT UNDER SIEGE

Chafing under British taxes, Newporters harassed British ships on several occasions during the 1760s and 1770s. When the Revolution broke out, the British decided to make an example of the port city, sailing 9,000 English militia and Hessian mercenaries into Newport Harbor in 1776. Those sympathetic to the revolutionary efforts fled to other parts of New England. In a matter of months, the permanent population declined from about 9,200 to 5,000.

Newport became a base of operations for the British army, who turned churches and civic buildings into their barracks and stables and imposed martial law under a stuffed-shirt British commander, General Richard Prescott (who was generally despised even by his own troops).

A glimmer of hope appeared in the form of French commander Count D'Estaing, who sailed into the harbor in summer 1778 with a small but potent fleet of ships, but a huge storm caused them to run for shelter. Even as a colonial militia attacked from Portsmouth, D'Estaing retreated out to sea and then all the way back to Boston. The Portsmouth rebels were left unsupported; disheartened, they retreated farther inland, only to encounter an even larger group of British troops along the way. A skirmish ensued, during which the Americans had at least a small victory, killing quite a few of the British before escaping to safety.

It wasn't until October 1779, when the British decided to bolster their defenses in New York, that they left the city. The day after the British evacuation, American troops returned to reoccupy what was left of Newport, confiscating property and transferring it to American owners. On July 12, Newporters prepared for a new, friendlier occupation when French General Rochambeau arrived in the city with more than 5,000 troops and a massive bounty of provisions.

Perhaps the most glorious day in Newport's still-young history occurred on March 6, 1781, when the commander-in-chief of the Continental Army, General George Washington, arrived by ship in Newport Harbor, debarking at Long Wharf clad in a full French uniform as a show of solidarity. A huge crowd of locals greeted the commander, and an exhilarating military parade was held on what is now Washington Square. The following evening Rochambeau, Washington, and the many other dignitaries celebrated their cooperative war effort with a lavish ball held in the still-standing Colony House on the square.

---

beginning of the Revolutionary War, when British forces decided to occupy Newport. From 1776 to 1779 the city remained firmly under British control. Most of the population, which was sympathetic to the war for independence, fled Newport, decimating trade. Even as it started to recover after the war, the shipping embargo imposed on New England during the War of 1812 effectively sealed Newport's fate as nothing more than a small-time port city.

For much of the 19th century, shipbuilding, naval exploits, and trade continued to play some role in Newport's fortunes, but Newport's greatest commodity continued to be its marvelous location at the tip of Aquidneck Island. Wealthy factory owners, rail and shipping tycoons, and other captains of industry began summering in this town that rarely became as hot in the summer as other parts of the Northeast. By the middle of the 19th century, almost any family with a big name, from Edith Wharton to the Vanderbilts, had a summer "cottage" (read: mansion) in the area south and east of downtown on Ocean Drive or Bellevue Avenue. And those who didn't had friends to visit here and were thus still a part of the town's culture. Since then, everyone from President Kennedy to Billy Joel has had homes here.

The city's brief stint as a pleasure village took a hit during the Depression. As fortunes fell and a spirit of fiscal conservatism took hold through World War II, many of Newport's mansions fell empty and were sold and subdivided into

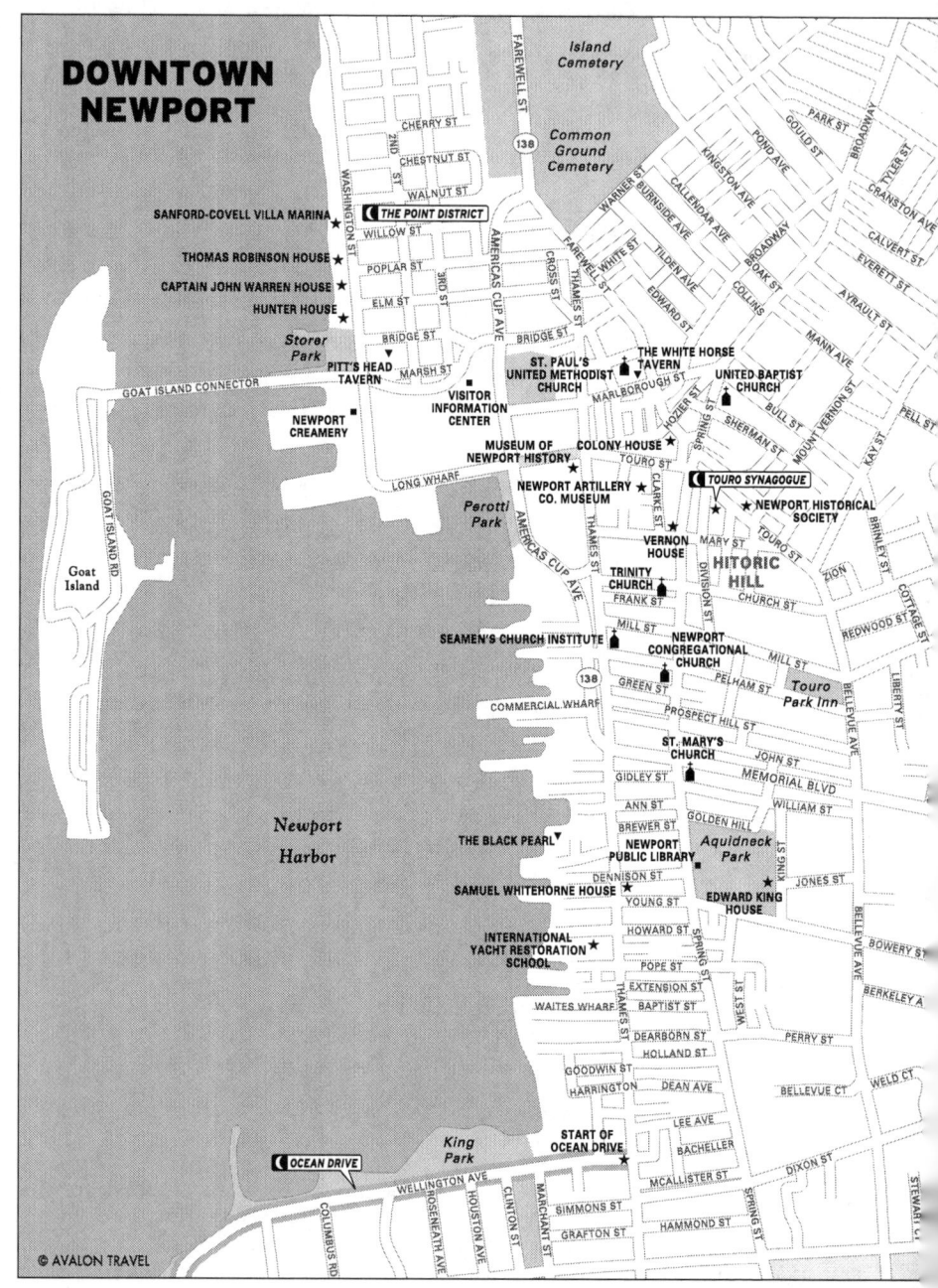

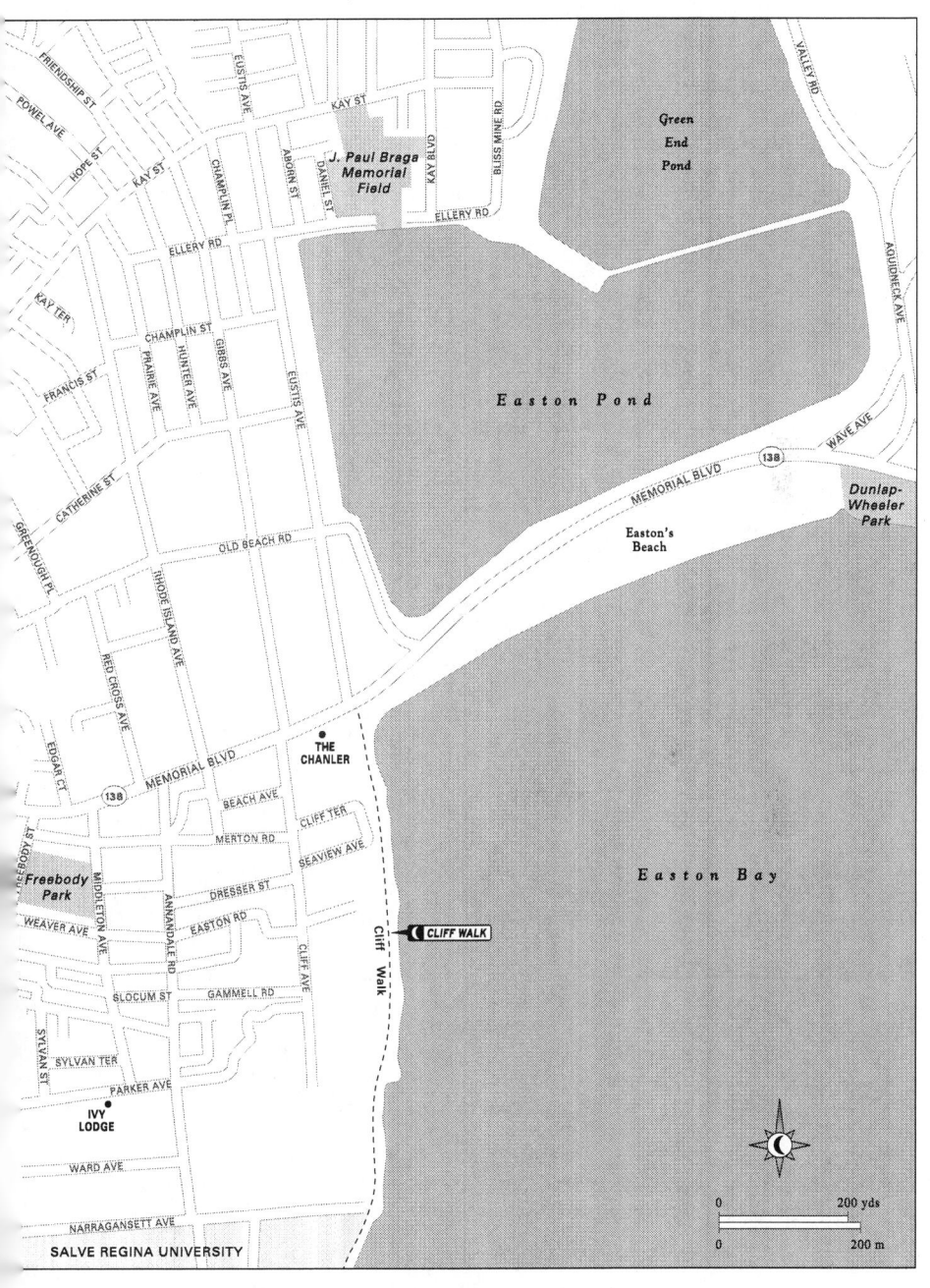

apartments, while others were shuttered completely. As weeklong summer vacations became increasingly popular with middle-class families after World War II, however, an increasing number of visitors began spending summers in Newport, and even more did so in the several motels just outside the city in Middletown.

Newport enjoyed a slow but steady resurgence from this point forward. Locals began to look around more and notice the city's incredible bounty of notable architecture, first by working toward the preservation of the city's grand "summer cottages." In 1967, tobacco heiress Doris Duke and others formed the Newport Restoration Foundation, which helped to preserve hundreds of important colonial houses. By the 1980s, one of Newport's oldest intact neighborhoods, the Point District, had become quite fashionable, its many 18th-century homes repainted and restored. For at least the past 30 years, Newport has enjoyed a reputation as a yachting hub, an increasingly upscale vacation destination, and a favorite place for touring magnificent homes.

## PLANNING YOUR TIME

Newport is the most popular destination in the state, and you'll want to spend at least a weekend here to touch on the major sights and activities. It is possible, though less than ideal, to see Newport in one day by touring Ocean Drive, walking the waterfront, and taking in at least one mansion tour. But of all the communities in Rhode Island, this is one where you should try to dedicate at least two full days.

Newport is really two cities in one—there's the tightly laid out downtown with its narrow one-way streets and rows of buildings dating from colonial through Victorian times, and then there's the sweeping, wealthy peninsula that juts south and east of all this, where expensive homes on large plots of land dominate the landscape. One full day to tour each of these areas, along with a little time set aside for the beach or a sail, is an ideal way to spend a weekend.

The catch is that Newport can be crowded in summer and on weekends just about any time of year, and hotel rates are among the highest in New England, so consider staying nearby and making several daytrips into town. Moderately priced motels and hotels are in nearby Middletown, where it's also not hard to find reasonably priced eateries. Still, there's no way of getting around the fact that summer is a favorite time to visit but an awful time for parking, getting a table quickly at restaurants, and enjoying the city's many house-museums and attractions without enduring long lines. Consider visiting during shoulder seasons of May or September, or on a weekday, when you'll have much more elbow room for exploring.

# Sights

## DOWNTOWN AND THE HARBOR

While the mansions and beaches are Newport's biggest attractions, the downtown waterfront has and irresistible draw. It's difficult to say what holds the bigger appeal: gawking at the chorus line of blinding white yachts moored in the harbor, or admiring the crush of humanity that fills the cobblestone wharfs on summer afternoons. A good place to start is the **Newport Visitors Information Center** (23 America's Cup Ave., 800/976-5122, www.gonewport.com), which is unusually comprehensive and useful. It is right at the northern entrance to downtown, adjacent to the city's bus terminal and the centrally located Newport Marriott. It's an excellent place to begin your explorations of the city, and it has a large pay-parking lot and garage, making it a good spot to ditch your wheels. Newport's downtown and harbor area can be managed easily on foot, and you can take public transportation from the visitors center to other parts of the city, including Ocean Drive and the mansions down on Bellevue Avenue.

## ◖ Touro Synagogue

Rhode Island's famous religious tolerance is symbolically—and beautifully—enshrined in Touro Synagogue (60 Touro St., 401/847-4794, www.tourosynagogue.org, 9:30 A.M.–4:30 P.M. Sun.–Wed. and Fri., 9:30 A.M.–7 P.M. Thurs. July–early Sept., 10 A.M.–2:30 P.M. Sun.–Fri. Sept.–Oct., $12 adults, $8 children under 13). Not only is it the oldest Jewish house of worship in the United States, it's also one of the most impressive 18th-century buildings in New England. Like so many historic buildings on the Eastern Seaboard, the synagogue's brochure brags that George Washington spent time here—in fact, it was here that he declared the new nation's position on religious freedom, pledging he would "give to bigotry no sanction, to persecution no assistance." If that connection helps draw visitors who might not otherwise venture into a synagogue, OK then, but Touro Synagogue should be on every visitor's short list of Newport attractions for its own historical, religious, and architectural significance.

In the mid-17th century, Sephardic Jews from Portugal and Spain caught wind of Roger Williams's Rhode Island colony and its unyielding tolerance of people of all religious persuasions. A small group of Jews arrived on Newport soil in the 1650s and formed a small congregation that met for decades in private homes and other temporary spaces. Eventually, the Newport Jews made plans to construct a synagogue, given a boost when one of the young nation's most prominent architects, Peter Harrison, volunteered to design it. The congregation, which chose the name Yeshaut Israel (Salvation of Israel), broke ground in 1759, roughly a century after the first Sephardim had arrived.

The design presented some unusual challenges for Harrison, who was forced to adapt his Georgian ideals to accommodate Sephardic traditions. Located on an inconspicuous side street, as custom dictated, the building stands diagonally on its plot so worshipers could face eastward in prayer towards Jerusalem. The exterior design is elegant but austere, and inside

Touro Synagogue features elaborate and symbolic architecture.

## EARLY NEWPORT'S QUAKER AND JEWISH GROUPS

Newport's enviable strategic position and all of Rhode Island's religious and political tolerance were not lost on persecuted people elsewhere in the New World and in Europe. Quakers were among the earliest and most numerous settlers; a shipload of them arrived in 1657, and in a short time many of Newport's most prominent citizens joined the Friends movement, among them William Coddington and Governor William Brenton (for whom Brenton Point, at the southwest tip of the city, is named). While Rhode Island was founded by Baptists, the state's first two centuries saw the election of more Quakers than adherents of any other religion.

Quakers were feared and despised elsewhere in New England. In fact, Mary Dyer, a Quaker and the wife of the secretary of Rhode Island, was hanged in Boston in 1660 after having been warned not to proselytize.

The second-oldest Jewish congregation in the United States was established in Newport (the first was formed four years earlier in New York City). In 1658 a ship containing 15 Sephardic Jewish families arrived from Barbados (having come originally from Spain and Portugal) and immediately formed a small congregation that would be formally named Jeshuat Israel a century later. They worshiped in private homes for many years until 1763, when they built the Touro Synagogue, the oldest synagogue in the United States. Newport's Jews also established what many believe is the first Freemasons lodge in the New World. Jews also immigrated to Rhode Island during the colonial era from Curaçao and later from Portugal. New England's whaling industry was begun by Jacob Rodrigues Rivera, who fled Spain during the Inquisition in the 1740s.

Early Jews were among the first and most successful pioneers of Newport industry, and had the British not occupied the city during the Revolutionary War, they might very well have helped steer the city to unrivaled economic growth. Instead, industry died with British occupation, and most of the city's Jews fled to colonies loyal to the American Revolution.

---

there is a sumptuous chamber supported by 12 Ionic columns that represent the ancient tribes of Israel. These columns support an upper gallery, from which 12 Corinthian columns reach skyward to support a domed ceiling. One of the most notable features of the interior is the five huge brass candle chandeliers that were donated by prominent Newport merchants during the 1760s. On the east side of the room stands the Holy Ark, which contains the Torah—the scrolls are hand-printed and set on wood rollers. Above this, the Ten Commandments are painted in Hebrew.

Four years after construction began, on December 2, 1763, Reb Isaac Touro led the first service in the synagogue that today bears his name. Interestingly, many non-Jews attended this first service, which is amazing considering the complete intolerance that not only Jews but all non-Congregationalists faced in most of the neighboring New England colonies. Shortly thereafter, however, the British occupation of Newport resulted in a near-abandonment of the city by most of its Jewish population, and services were discontinued. The road back to the building began in the mid-1800s, when Touro's sons, wealthy merchants Abraham and Judah, left immense fortunes upon their deaths to care for the structure, which eventually reopened in 1883. It has continued to operate in the Sephardic tradition of worship ever since.

Except on Saturdays and Jewish holidays, Touro Synagogue is generally open for tours 10 A.M.–4 P.M. daily in summer, with shorter hours the rest of the year. You can easily walk from here up Touro Street to the congregation's burial ground, where Judah Touro, Aaron Lopez, and other prominent members of the community are buried.

### Historic Hill

While Newport is best-known for the mansions constructed in the late 19th century, the town has historically significant buildings stretching back more than 200 years, many of which are clustered around the area west of the waterfront. Before setting foot in any of the mansions, culture and history buffs should take a detour to the **Museum of Newport History** (Thames St., at the bottom of Washington Sq., 401/841-8770 or 401/846-0813, www.newporthistorical.org, 10 A.M.–4:30 P.M. Tues.–Fri., by appointment Mon., shorter hours in winter, $4 adults, $2 children over 5), where the exhibits give a nice overview of the history of the city and southern Rhode Island. Housed in the historic Brick Market Place, the space is crammed with many artifacts that trace the city's history, including decorative pieces and artwork, vintage photos, and ship models. Other exhibits touch on the city's founding fathers, John Clarke and William Coddington, as well as on the indigenous Native Americans who lived here for many centuries and the diverse ethnic and religious makeup of Newport's earliest citizens, including Quakers, Jews, Portuguese, and African Americans.

May–mid-September a variety of guided walking tours (401/841-8770, www.newporthistorytours.org, $12 adults, $5 children under 12) that focus on the city's history leave from the museum. Themes include Jewish Newport, Colonial Newport, and pirate tours.

The **Newport Historical Society** (82 Touro St., 401/846-0813, www.newporthistorical.org, 9:30 A.M.–4:30 P.M. Mon.–Fri., 9:30 A.M.–noon Sat., free admission), home to Newport's historic **Seventh Day Baptist Meeting House,** the first home of the Seventh Day Baptists, is a rather simple building that dates to 1730, when it was designed by Richard Munday. It looks far more like a house than a place of worship. The Newport Historical Society, founded in 1854, bought the building in the 1880s and has used it as its headquarters ever since, although the actual offices and exhibit areas are in an addition behind the church.

The Historical Society also manages several other properties, both private homes and public buildings, that are well worth looking

Trinity Church overlooks Queen Anne Square.

into. The most significant is **Colony House** (Washington Sq., 11 A.M.–2:30 P.M. Thurs.–Sat. July–Aug., 11 A.M.–2:30 P.M. Sat. Sept.–Oct., or by appointment, $5 adults and seniors, $3 children), which dates to 1739. Here on May 4, 1776, the state assembly forswore its allegiance to the British crown, thus establishing Rhode Island as the young nation's first independent state exactly two months before the other 12 fell in line. It is the fourth-oldest existing building in the United States to have served as a state capitol, serving as one of the two Rhode Island State Houses until 1901, when the new State House in Providence opened. Architect Richard Munday, who's also responsible for the nearby Seventh Day Baptist Meeting House and Trinity Church, designed this Georgian-style building. Inside you'll find one of Rhode Islander Gilbert Stuart's famous portraits of George Washington.

Also in the vicinity of Washington Square is the 1846 **United Baptist Church, John Clarke Memorial** (30 Spring St., 401/847-3210, 8:30 A.M.–noon Mon.–Fri.), located to the north and east of Colony House. The congregation was established in Portsmouth in 1638 by pastor Dr. John Clarke, the very gentleman who obtained Rhode Island's Royal Charter in 1663 from King Charles II. For background on the Revolutionary War's Battle of Newport as well as other conflicts, visit the **Newport Artillery Co. Museum** (23 Clarke St., 401/846-8488, www.newportartillery.org, 10 A.M.–4 P.M. Sat. or by appointment, free admission), which is housed in a cut-granite Greek revival building just south of Washington Square on Clarke Street. Military objects and artifacts from more than 100 nations fill these rooms, including 15 cannons spanning 150 years, one of them struck by Paul Revere in 1798. Other unique military artifacts include uniforms worn by former general and Secretary of State Colin Powell, the Vietnam War's General Westmoreland, and Egyptian president Anwar Sadat.

A little farther down Clarke Street at the intersection of Mary Street is **Vernon House** (46 Clarke St., 401/849-7300, www.newportrestoration.org), a fine colonial house with a hipped roof. It served as headquarters for Rochambeau, the commander of French expeditionary forces during the Revolutionary War, who assumed control of the house in 1780 after British forces ceded the city. In this building in early March 1781, he and George Washington reportedly planned the Continental Army's coup de grâce against the British at the Battle of Yorktown. The home is now managed by the Newport Restoration Foundation as a private residence, although it is open to scholars by special appointment.

Another notable historic home nearby is the Newport Historical Society's **Wanton-Lyman-Hazard House** (17 Broadway, 401/846-0813, www.newporthistorical.org, open for tours 11 A.M.–2:30 P.M. Thurs.–Sat. July–Aug., 11 A.M.–2:30 P.M. Sat. Sept.–Oct., or by appointment, $5 adults and seniors, $3 children under 12), which dates to 1675—it's one of the oldest restored houses in the state. The imposing house was built as the residence of wealthy sea captain Stephen Mumford, but the most famous owner was the former governor of Rhode Island (in 1741) Richard Ward, and the house takes its name from members of the family that occupied the house 1782–1911. Several additions were made to the house during its first 100 years, including the fine interior crown molding and wood paneling. The society has also worked with the Newport Garden Club to restore its gardens, which include an interpretive colonial herb garden.

Just around the corner, near the corner of Farewell and Marlborough Streets, the **Great Friends Meeting House** (401/846-0813, www.newporthistorical.org, 11 A.M.–2:30 P.M. Thurs.–Sat. July–Aug., 11 A.M.–2:30 P.M. Sat. Sept.–Oct., or by appointment, $4) was once the largest and most prominent building in Newport, visible to ships arriving in Newport Harbor from some way out. With parts dating back to 1699, it is the oldest surviving house of worship in town and was expanded continuously over the subsequent two centuries. Quakers used it as the setting for the New England Yearly Meetings. The Society of Friends was an important influence on Newport society during the 17th and 18th centuries, a time when the then-radical religion was harshly persecuted in other parts of the New World. Newport Quaker Nicholas Easton was elected governor of Rhode Island in 1672; he helped push through the young land's earliest known conscientious-objector law, which allowed any citizen to turn down military enlistment if his religion forbade him from fighting.

In addition to the single admission charge for each of its properties ($5 for adults), Newport Historical offers a package deal with admission to Colony House, Wanton-Lyman-Hazard House, and Great Friends Meeting House for $12.

Nearby is **St. Paul's United Methodist Church** (12 Marlborough St.), whose congregation dates to 1800. The church was built six years later, becoming the first Methodist church in the world with a steeple, a bell, and fixed pews. Having opened in 1687, the **White Horse Tavern** (26 Marlborough St.,

401/849-3600, 11:30 A.M.–2:30 P.M. and 6–9 P.M. Mon.–Fri., noon–3 P.M. and 6–9 P.M. Sat.–Sun.) is said to be the oldest extant tavern in the United States, and it still operates as a restaurant. During the state's early history, when Newport was the capital, members of the Rhode Island Assembly often convened in the tavern.

If you haven't yet tired of churches, one of the grandest in Newport is **Trinity Church** (1 Queen Anne Sq., 401/846-0360, www.trinitynewport.org, 10 A.M.–1 P.M. Mon.–Fri. May–mid-June, 10 A.M.–4 P.M. Mon.–Fri. mid-June–early July, 10 A.M.–4 P.M. daily early July–Aug., 10 A.M.–1 P.M. Mon.–Fri. Sept.–mid-Oct., 10 A.M.–4 P.M. Mon.–Fri. mid-late Oct., services 8 A.M. and 10 A.M. Sun. and noon Wed. year-round), dramatically overlooking leafy Queen Anne Square. The elegant building dates to 1726 and is modeled after the London churches designed by famed British architect Christopher Wren. With its lofty white spire, this dignified building is one of Newport's most recognizable and impressive structures. Definitely try to peek inside to see the only three-tiered, center-aisle, glass pulpit in the country. For the obligatory George Washington connection, take a look at pew number 81, in which the first president once worshiped. Tours are given every Sunday following the 10 A.M. Episcopal service.

Two blocks south on Spring Street is another of Newport's elegant places of worship, the **Newport Congregational Church** (73 Pelham St., 401/849-2238, www.newportcongregationalchurch.org, 9 A.M.–noon Mon.–Sat., services 10 A.M. Sun.). This 1880 structure is one of only two churches left standing in the United States with an interior designed entirely by noted architect John La Farge, who also perfected the technique for creating the opalescent glass used in the windows. On the interior walls are elaborate and colorful murals.

## The Waterfront

Down the hill, more shops and restaurants line the eastern portion of Thames Street, while wharves jut into Newport Harbor across the

a summer scene on a Newport wharf

street. These wharves now contain a mix of businesses, restaurants, and hotels. You might stop at the **Seamen's Church Institute** (18 Market Sq., just off Thames St., 401/847-4260, 6 A.M.–6 P.M. daily) to catch your breath and to admire this handsome building that has served the needs of seafarers for nearly a century. The building contains a small nondenominational chapel, a café, public restrooms with a coin laundry and showers, a library, and a small museum (with limited hours; call ahead). After merging with America's Cup Avenue to become a broad and busy road for a few blocks, Thames Street once again becomes a narrow one-way street with an easy and quaint pace past Commercial Wharf.

A block up Memorial Drive from the intersection with Thames Street is **St. Mary's Church** (Spring St. at Memorial Blvd., Mass 8 A.M., 9:30 A.M., and 11 A.M. Sun., 5 P.M. Sat., 7:30 A.M. Mon.–Fri.), which houses the oldest Catholic parish in the state, established in 1828. The present church dates to 1852 and is considered one of the finest examples of Gothic revival architecture on the Eastern Seaboard, but the building's real claim to fame is having served as the setting for the wedding of John F. Kennedy and Jacqueline Bouvier on September 12, 1953.

Just south and a block east of Thames Street is leafy Aquidneck Park, bounded by Spring, Golden Hill, King, and Bowery Streets. Adjoining the park is the imposing **Newport Public Library** (300 Spring St., 401/847-8720, www.newportlibraryri.org, 11 A.M.–8 P.M. Mon., 9 A.M.–8 P.M. Tues.–Thurs., 9 A.M.–6 P.M. Fri.–Sat.), a general-purpose facility that also has some impressive special collections on Newport history, U.S. history, cookbooks, African American studies, Chinese culture, and Chinese-language books. Also facing the park is the imposing **Edward King House** (35 King St., 401/846-7426), one of the finest examples of Italianate villa design in the United States. Designed by noted architect Richard Upjohn, it was the largest house in Newport when it was built in 1847 for China Trade merchant Edward King, presaging the elaborate Newport mansions that were to follow several decades later. Today the building is a seniors center. While there are no formal tours, visitors are welcome to look around at the opulent interior.

While Newport has many homes and museums from the colonial and Victorian periods, the only house-museum from the Federal period is the **Samuel Whitehorne House** (416 Thames St., 401/847-2448, 11 A.M.–3 P.M. Thurs.–Mon. May–Oct., $6 adults, free for children under 12), a few blocks down Thames Street. The property is overseen by the **Newport Restoration Foundation** (51 Touro St., 401/849-7300, www.newport-restoration.com), an organization founded by the late heiress Doris Duke, who assembled an incomparable collection of Federal and colonial pieces from Newport's top cabinetmakers. She placed much of the collection in this house, which dates to 1811 and originally belonged to one of Newport's most successful shipping merchants, Samuel Whitehorne, who earned his fortune in rum distilling, shipping, and—although it's not documented conclusively—the slave trade. The house has all the classic elements of Federal architecture: a symmetrical hipped roof, a lavish formal garden, and a circular entryway. Guided tours are offered at 10:30 A.M. and 3 P.M. Thursday–Monday in summer for $12 pp. A $30 combination ticket is available to tour both the Whitehorne House and Duke's former estate at Rough Point.

While Newport has more than its share of restored homes and public buildings, only here could there also be an organization dedicated to the restoration of nautical craft. The **International Yacht Restoration School** (449 Thames St., 401/848-5777, ext. 227, www.iyrs.org, 10 A.M.–5 P.M., Wed.–Mon., tours at 1 P.M., free) is a nonprofit organization whose mission is to teach the "skills, history, and science needed to construct, restore, and maintain classic watercraft." Regardless of your own knowledge and experience with classic boats, you might just stop in to check out the school's impressive collection of fine old boats, including the IYRS flagship, the *Coronet,* which has sailed around the world and hosted such luminaries as Alexander Graham Bell and the king of Hawaii. A trip here makes a great prelude to checking out the Museum of Yachting at Fort Adams; a free shuttle makes the trip between the two properties.

## ◖ THE POINT DISTRICT

The Point District, which has one of New England's finest concentrations of colonial architecture, extends from just north of the Newport Visitors Center north to the Newport Bridge. It's a thoroughly engaging neighborhood for a stroll, its narrow streets packed with colonial and later Victorian homes, most of them painted in traditional Newport blues, slates, brick reds, mustards, and creams.

A highlight of the neighborhood is **Hunter House** (54 Washington St., 401/847-1000, www.newportmansions.org, tours 10 A.M.–5 P.M. daily late June–late Sept., $25), which sits at the southwest edge of the Point District near the bridge to Goat Island. This 1748 slate-gray Georgian mansion contains a priceless collection of 18th-century furnishings, ceramics, silver, pewter, and ornately carved woodwork. While Hunter House is the only home here open to the public, it's worth taking the time to see the dozens of wonderfully preserved homes by strolling the dozen or so blocks up Washington Street along the waterfront about as far as the Newport Bridge, then back down 2nd Street, which runs parallel a block east.

Just a block east of Hunter House is the **Pitt's Head Tavern** (77 Bridge St.), which is actually not original to the neighborhood. This 1724 gambrel-roofed building was built on Washington Square but moved here in the mid-1960s. Back on Washington Street and north past Hunter House is a pair of distinctive buildings, the 1736 **Captain John Warren House** (62 Washington St.), notable for its elegant central fanlight front door, and the **Thomas Robinson House** (64 Washington St.), owned by generations of the same family for two centuries. Just a bit farther north is the **Sanford-Covell Villa Marina** (72 Washington St., 401/847-0206 or 866/916-0206), a towering Victorian mansion designed by leading 19th-cenutry architect William Ralph Emerson; it's now a bed-and-breakfast.

## BROADWAY

An untouristy but increasingly hip neighborhood that begins on the eastern edge of downtown and extends northeast into Middletown, Broadway is everything that the rest of Newport is not: slightly countercultural, highly quirky, and offbeat. You can understand why some locals refer to it as the East Village of Newport. Broadway is a repository of thrift shops, trendy but inexpensive eateries, affable pubs, and piercing parlors—it's the city's nod to Wickenden Street in Providence, and a refreshing change of pace when you become tired of seeing hordes of tourists and neatly preened yachters.

## ◖ OCEAN DRIVE

One of the most famous scenic drives on the East Coast, 9.5-mile Ocean Drive is a roughly C-shaped route that begins at the lower end of downtown, on Wellington Avenue at the intersection with Thames Street. Ocean Drive isn't one road but rather the name of a well-marked route that connects several roads. At least half the fun of this journey, which can take from an hour to half a day, depending on how often you stop, is simply peering out the window at the stunning homes, sandy beaches, and ocean vistas.

Still right in town on Newport Harbor, you'll pass little **King Park** on your right as you drive west along Wellington Avenue; this is the city's small but pleasant in-town beach. About one mile farther along, you'll come to a National Historic Landmark and one of the most formidable coastal forts ever built in the United States, **Fort Adams** (Eisenhower House, Fort Adams State Park, 401/841-0707, www.fortadams.org, 10 A.M.–4 P.M. daily late May–mid-Oct., grounds admission free, fortification tours $10 adults, $5 youths 6–17, free for children under 6, $25 families). The fort served the region from the 1820s through World War II, occupying a grassy point opposite downtown Newport, about a mile across Newport Harbor. Today you can tour the bastions, officers quarters, the enclosed 6.25-acre parade, and the exterior dry moat that helped prevent the fort from ever being compromised by an enemy. Entrance to the main fortification is by guided tour only, but admission to the grounds is free.

Also located at Fort Adams State Park, the **Museum of Yachting** (Fort Adams State Park, 401/847-1018, www.moy.org, 10 A.M.–5 P.M. daily late May–Sept., $5 adults, free for students and children under 18) documents Newport's legacy as one of the world's great centers for boating. Exhibits include the impact of Newport's Gilded Age on the city's reputation as a yachting center as well as an America's Cup Gallery, where photos and records document the races since the 1930s. Different events are held throughout the year, including the Classic Yacht Regatta on Labor Day weekend and several smaller regattas and events.

On leaving the park, continue back onto Harrison Avenue. Although it's no longer open to the public, **Hammersmith Farm** (off

Harrison Ave., next to Fort Adams State Park) is home to an 1887 mansion that is one of Newport's most fabled properties. The site of Jacqueline Bouvier and John F. Kennedy's wedding reception in 1953, it became the "summer White House" for the first family after Kennedy became president. Once open for tours, the house was sold for $8 million to a private owner in 1999.

A short distance farther along Harrison Avenue, make a right onto Ridge Road and follow it around, passing the elegant Ocean Cliff Hotel. This road meets with Castle Hill Avenue, from which a small lane leads to the **Castle Hill Coast Guard Station** (75 Ridge Rd., 401/846-3676, tours by appointment during daylight hours). Back on the main route, you'll finally reach Ocean Avenue, which runs right along the water with mostly contemporary and colonial-style beach homes on the inland side of the street.

Where Ocean Drive turns nearly 90 degrees around Brenton Point, you'll find a parking area for **Brenton Point State Park** (401/849-4562 May–Oct., 401/847-2400 year-round, www.riparks.com/brenton.htm), a rugged, rocky promontory overlooking the ocean. You can picnic here or stroll along the beach, and it's phenomenally popular for kite-flying.

Continue on Ocean Drive along the waterfront back toward Newport, passing the Newport Country Club, some private beaches, and several gorgeous homes that range from century-old Victorian castles to rather recently built compounds with lavish decking and many-gabled roofs. Officially, Ocean Drive ends at Coggeshall Avenue, where a left turn will bring you back into lower downtown, about two miles away. Make a right turn, however, and after following the road a short way, make a left onto Bellevue Avenue to begin a tour of the Newport mansions of the Gilded Age—in the reverse direction from most visitors, who approach the mansions from town.

## ◖ ROUGH POINT

Some people get rich for being famous; other are famous for being rich. Heiress Doris Duke—the title is practically part of her name—belongs to the latter category. In 1925, when she was just 12 years old, she inherited $100 million on the death of her father, a tobacco and electricity magnate. She led a colorful life, to say the least, traveling around the world, working as a foreign correspondent during World War II, and famously romancing a number of men, marrying and divorcing three of them. Today, her legacy is best seen in the field of historic preservation through her establishment of the Newport Restoration Foundation, which started the city's preservation boom in the 1960s. Since then, it has helped fully restore more than 80 threatened structures in Newport, including the mansion where Duke herself spent the summers, Rough Point (680 Bellevue Ave., 401/847-8344, www.newportrestoration.com, tours by appointment 9:45 A.M.–3:45 P.M. mid-May–early Nov., $25 adults, free for children under 13).

A grand mansion built in 1889 for Frederick W. Vanderbilt, the home occupies a rocky point overlooking the ocean. James B. Duke, Doris's father, bought the estate in 1922 but lived in it for just three years before his death. Inside, you'll find a collection of rare Ming vases and ceramics, plus original paintings by Renoir, Van Dyck, and portraitist Joshua Reynolds. There is also a phenomenal collection of furniture and antiquities, rare among Newport mansions.

Rough Point can be visited only by guided tour, which are offered regularly at the Gateway Visitors Center, or you can book online at www.newportrestoration.com; only a limited number of tickets are sold each day, so it's highly advisable to buy tickets online well in advance, especially on summer weekends. The upside is that the tours are limited to just 12 people, making for a more intimate experience.

A new exhibit explores the life of Doris Duke and her efforts to preserve Newport's homes. It's included with the cost of the tour, or visitors can visit it on its own (1–4 P.M. Thurs. and Sat., $5).

## BELLEVUE AVENUE

Running parallel to Thames Street a few blocks east and up the hill from Newport Harbor, Bellevue Avenue had become a wealthy, exclusive retreat by the time of the Civil War. Each season, new arrivals built ever-larger summer cottages until development peaked around 1890–1914, generally referred to as Newport's Gilded Age. During these 25 years, unbelievably wealthy industrialists and high-society types built massive, fortresslike homes and threw parties that sometimes cost more than $250,000 a pop. Many of the grandest of these houses still stand today, operated as house-museums and open to the public—a legacy that Newport's self-important summer bigwigs would have deemed unacceptable.

As stunning as the mansions are, they are not the only sights along Bellevue Avenue. North of the intersection with Memorial Boulevard is the **Redwood Library** (50 Bellevue Ave., 401/847-0292, www.redwoodlibrary.org, 9:30 A.M.–5:30 P.M. Mon., Wed., and Fri.–Sat., 9:30 A.M.–8 P.M. Thurs., 1–5 P.M. Sun.), a neoclassical structure built in 1750 by one of the nation's first architects, Peter Harrison, and once frequented by Gilbert Stuart, William and Henry James, and Edith Wharton. Tours of the library are given at 10:30 A.M. Monday–Friday, but the public is welcome to visit anytime during regular library hours.

Just a block south and across the street is the **Newport Art Museum** (76 Bellevue Ave., 401/848-8200, www.newportartmuseum.org, 10 A.M.–5 P.M. Tues.–Sat., noon–5 P.M. Sun. May–Oct., 10 A.M.–4 P.M. Tues.–Sat., noon–4 P.M. Sun. Nov.–Apr., $10 adults, $8 seniors, $6 students, free for children under 5), which shows the works of mostly regional artists, running the gamut from American impressionism to modern sculpture. Much of the work is quite good, especially the evocative seascapes by members of the Provincetown or Gloucester schools of artists in the same league (if without quite the same artistry) as Winslow Homer. Colonial-era portraits line the stairway of the Griswold House, the older of the two buildings. Across a sculpture-studded field, the

The Newport Art Museum features the work of regional artists.

Cushing House stages changing exhibits, some of them quite clever: A recent exhibition, for example, focused on Newport's connection to Japan, which was opened to U.S. trade in the 19th century by the city's own Commodore Matthew Perry; items on display included a full suit of samurai armor.

Across Bellevue Avenue and down Mill Street is the **Old Stone Mill,** which anchors Touro Park. Much controversy surrounds this structure, which many locals had believed was built by Vikings 1,000 years ago, until improved forensic research cast doubt on this explanation. Another story is that one of the city's earliest residents and Rhode Island's first governor, Benedict Arnold, built the structure sometime in the 18th century.

### International Tennis Hall of Fame

Tennis may have originated in England, but in the United States its history passes through Newport. The first U.S. National Lawn Tennis Championship, later known as the U.S. Open, was played on the grass-lawn tennis courts of the Newport Casino in 1881. Now that hallowed ground has become the International Tennis Hall of Fame and Museum (194 Bellevue Ave., 401/849-3990 or 800/457-1144, www.tennisfame.org, 9:30 A.M.–5 P.M. daily, $11 admission includes court access). Just south of Memorial Boulevard, the museum contains about a dozen exhibit rooms displaying memorabilia of the game, including an Andy Warhol portrait of Chris Evert, the original 1874 tennis patent granted by the queen of England to Major Walter Clopton Wingfield, and a gallery celebrating tennis champions of the early 20th century. The museum is unusual in that it remains a working tennis facility that's open to the public for play; this is the only lawn tennis facility in the country that's not a private club. There's also quite an extensive gift shop as well as a restaurant overlooking the courts.

### National Museum of American Illustration

Just a bit farther south is the National Museum of American Illustration (NMAI,

the grass courts at the International Tennis Hall of Fame

## A BRIEF HISTORY OF TENNIS

Tennis is an extremely old game, with roots in 11th-century France, and also a rather modern game – its present form dates to around the 1870s, when many wealthy Brits installed courts at their country manors. Similarly, as a wealthy leisure class was emerging in the United States, especially in New England, interest in tennis increased there.

In 1874, British Major Walter Clopton Wingfield devised a new form of tennis that combined the centuries-old game, which is now generally referred to as "court tennis" or "real tennis," with some characteristics of badminton, which has Native American origins. This variation, called lawn tennis, is the true ancestor of the game we play today, while real tennis is a comparatively obscure game played in few places.

Just a few years after its introduction to high society in New York, the first men's tennis championship in the United States was held at the Newport Casino; a women's championship was added in 1887. International competitions began in 1900 with the Davis Cup, which started as a men's tourney between the United States and England, although tennis had already developed a strong following in Australia, France, Holland, and many other nations.

Although tennis was something of a blueblooded country-club activity during its first half century, its popularity spread to the general public during, ironically, the Depression, when a number of federally funded New Deal programs led to the construction of tennis courts at public parks and schools.

Professional tennis, of course, has enjoyed an almost meteoric rise in popularity through the past three decades. One of the four major tournaments, the U.S. Open is the modern-day descendant of that first championship held in Newport in 1881. For about 35 years, the Newport Casino and its illustrious tournament served as the U.S. equivalent of Wimbledon, and it might still today if not for Newport's relative isolation from the Northeast's major population centers. In 1915, the U.S. Open was shifted from Newport to Long Island, New York.

Nevertheless, from 1915 onward an invitational tournament continued to be staged on Newport's grass court, and in 1954 the Newport Casino was converted into the home of the National Tennis Hall of Fame. Starting in 1976, the Newport Casino has hosted the Hall of Fame Tennis Championship (now sponsored by Campbell's Soup), the only pro tournament in the nation still played only on grass courts.

492 Bellevue Ave., 401/851-8949, www.americanillustration.org, 11 A.M.–4:30 P.M. Sat.–Sun. late May–early Sept. or by appointment year-round for a minimum of 8 visitors, $18 adults, $16 seniors, $12 children 5–12, free for children under 5), which is worth admiring from the outside and also interesting to tour, keeping in mind the limited hours of admission. This museum is housed in one of the grand mansions along Bellevue Avenue, the 1898 Vernon Court, which is modeled after a 17th-century château. John Merven Carrère and Thomas Hastings, also responsible for the New York Public Library and the Frick Collection, designed the mansion, noted for its marble Great Hall and its steep roof punctuated by nine tall chimneys. The museum was formed with a mission to preserve and present the nation's finest illustrated art—works commissioned to appear in magazines, books, advertisements, and other print products. The collection displays work by dozens of famous illustrators, among them Maxfield Parrish, Norman Rockwell, N. C. Wyeth, Charles Dana Gibson, Howard Chandler Christy, and many others. As you tour the mansion you'll also see a vast array of decorative arts and period furnishings.

### Salve Regina University

Just off the east side of Bellevue Avenue is the attractive campus of Salve Regina University (Ochre Point Ave., 401/847-6650, www.salve.

## THE GILDED AGE

Around 1850, real estate speculators began buying up the land south and east of downtown, and Bellevue Avenue was extended south toward the water. This development triggered the period of wealth in Newport that would come to be known as "The Gilded Age." Wealthy New Yorkers and Bostonians began building summer cottages in this new section of Newport, and each summer the newest structures dwarfed the previous ones both in size and opulence. Many Southerners also built homes in this increasingly exclusive summer colony. The value of land skyrocketed, and the boom continued through the late 1850s.

After a short-lived recession, civic leaders decided to throw a sumptuous party for summering bigwigs as well as the many past Newport residents who had not been back for some time. The ball was a huge success, and the tradition of summer entertaining continued to grow each subsequent year. Predictably, the Civil War interrupted Newport's growth as a resort, but as soon as it ended, grand summer life in Newport returned stronger than ever.

This time, the ranks of summer residents included visibly fewer Southerners and many more wealthy families from Boston, New York, and Philadelphia. Local society movers and shakers included Mrs. Nicholas Beach, who hosted well-attended dance balls; Ward McAlister, who popularized the tradition of sumptuous picnics; and Mrs. August Belmont, who threw over-the-top dinner parties. For several weeks every summer, these rituals of entertaining on the grandest scale were embedded in Newport's regimen, as the very wealthiest hosts sought to outdo one another.

Into the 1880s, the presence of Newport's superrich part-time residents began to pay off in the form of significant investments in infrastructure improvements. A city water system was inaugurated in 1881, and private telephone service came the following year. Electric trolley service, which ran from Commercial Wharf up over Bath Street (now Memorial Boulevard) to Easton's Beach, became a reality in 1889. Upper-class leisure activities also made inroads during these years, with the earliest national tennis matches commencing in 1881, followed by polo and then golf tournaments. The little city by the sea, virtually bereft of industry or commercial clout, became a powerhouse owing to its sterling reputation as a playground for the rich and famous.

The ostentation hit its peak beginning in the next decade. As recorded in the Works Progress Administration guidebook on Rhode Island, which was written in 1937, "probably America will never again see such lavish entertaining as took place at Newport during the summer seasons of the 'gilded years,' 1890-1914. Into six or seven weeks each season were crowded balls, dinners, and parties of every description.... Huge sums were

edu). There are 18 historically significant buildings on the property, which is a few blocks east of Bellevue Cliff Walk. The school is heavily involved in preservation programs, sponsoring lectures and preservation events and working hard to preserve its many prominent structures. The most famous building on campus is perhaps **Ochre Court,** one of the city's earliest grand summer cottages, completed in 1892 with a design by Richard Morris Hunt. Ochre Court was donated in 1947 to serve as the foundation of Salve Regina, and through the past few decades, several other summer cottages in the adjoining neighborhood have been donated to the school. Noted architects whose works are now part of the campus include H. H. Richardson, the father of Richardsonian Romanesque; Charles Eamer Kempe; and the firm of McKim, Mead, and White. Designers who have worked on these homes and grounds include Louis Comfort Tiffany and Frederick Law Olmsted. You can walk through the main floor of Ochre Court, which serves as the school's main administrative offices, 9 A.M.–4 P.M. Monday–Friday; there's no admission charge, but keep in mind that this isn't a formal house-museum with tour guides.

spent in the prevailing spirit of rivalry. Mrs. Pembroke Jones set aside $300,000 at the beginning of every Newport season for entertaining, and some hostesses spent even more. Sometimes a single ball cost $100,000." Even by the outlandish standards of today, as evidenced by multimillion-dollar Hollywood weddings, the social excesses in Newport remain unmatched.

Looking back, it's hard to imagine that most of these very rich Newporters even derived much pleasure from their wealth or their social standing. The jockeying for favorable social position was a blood sport, and it's supposed that many an upper-class family in the United States avoided Newport altogether, unwilling or unable to compete in this major league of snobbery and self-aggrandizement.

Newport year-rounders, sneeringly called "footstools" by the elite, despised the summer "cottagers," all the while, in many cases, undertaking their lowliest chores. A slightly higher class of full-time residents made out rather well, running shops or offering services and gouging the summer-comers for all they could; they had absolutely no shame in attempting to live well off these unbelievably rich visitors. And there was almost no interplay between the summer visitors and the full-time Newporters – even streetcars were not allowed to travel along Bellevue and Ocean Avenues.

In the Gilded Age, Harry Lehr and Mrs. William Astor became the leading society players in Newport, more or less controlling every aspect of the social season, determining who could move in the city's most desirable circles and who should be kept down. The so-called "400," a social precursor of sorts to today's Forbes 500, were those individuals fortunate enough to attend the ball held each summer in the ballroom of the Astor home. The room accommodated 400, and so Harry Lehr and Mrs. Astor pored over the *Social Register* each year to arrive at a definitive guest list. To be on this list could easily legitimize a person's social standing; to be excluded from it could scar one's reputation irreparably.

The outrageous antics of Newport's society mavens gradually began to wear on those outside looking in, most significantly the press. The gossip writers of the time took great glee in reporting each and every excess, from the time that Harry Lehr and Mrs. Stuyvesant Fish held a party at which a diminutive trained monkey was booked as the guest of honor, to the infamous dog gala, when Lehr invited about 100 canines and their owners to a lavish sit-down meal where thousands of dollars were spent on food. The public reaction to these displays was finally such that the summer party-throwers began to exercise more restraint, but the over-the-top parties still continued for many years.

## NEWPORT'S MANSIONS

Much has been written about Newport's vast marble halls, and not all of it positive. As the railroad and steel tycoons began constructing their ostentatious summer homes at the end of the 19th century, they symbolized a new Renaissance in American architecture. Finally, the New World would have palaces to rival those of the Old World—built not by kings but by captains of industry. And while they might give a nod to the classical forms of Europe in style, they implemented the most advanced technology—electric lighting, hot and cold running water—that American ingenuity could conjure. Within a few short years, however, as the excesses of the Gilded Age spawned a Progressive backlash, no less an authority than novelist Henry James derided the Newport cottages as "white elephants"—beautiful but useless symbols of excess. Some modern architects have continued to turn up their noses at the extravagant tastes of the robber barons of the day, who seemed to choose the most garish forms of decoration in their homes that they could find.

Even knowing that, however, there's nothing like the impact of walking into some of these homes, whose every element seems calculated to impress. The Astors, Vanderbilts, and other millionaires of the time literally spared no expense in constructing their masterpieces, lavishing the same care and attention on these architectural endeavors as they did in constructing their multimillion-dollar businesses. While the initial reaction of most visitors is one of sheer overwhelmed amazement, closer inspection reveals countless pleasures in the details. There's not a single sconce or column that's free of adornment—each wall panel, and in some cases each ceiling tile, is decorated with some family crest or symbol designed to bless the fortunes of its creator. Even the most cynical viewer of the selfishness of wealth has to feel some awe in the beauty of so many well-thought design elements coming together in a harmonious whole. Lovers of antiques and historic homes may feel they've died and gone to architectural heaven.

The **Preservation Society of Newport County** (401/847-1000, www.newportmansions.org) operates tours of most of the houses. Several different tour possibilities are available, including combination tickets that provide a discount.

## Kingscote Mansion and the Isaac Bell House

The first mansion you find as you travel south down Bellevue Avenue is also historically one of the first to establish the trend of Newport as a summer vacation spot for the rich and powerful. Kingscote Mansion (Bowery Ave. at Bellevue Ave., 401/847-1000, www.newportmansions.org, 10 A.M.–4:30 P.M. daily late June–early Sept., $14 adults, $5 children 6–17, children under 6 free) was the brainchild of George Noble Jones, a wealthy Georgia plantation owner who wanted a grand seaside residence to escape the Southern heat during summer. He commissioned architect Richard Upjohn to build him a truly unique and modern residence—Upjohn's Gothic Revival cottage, all asymmetrical gables, dormers, and drip moldings, represented the cutting edge of English architecture at the time—a reaction against the staid classical forms of Greek Revival that were otherwise in vogue. Today the home stands as one of the only examples of its style and size. Completed in 1841, Kingscote set the tone that other mansions were to follow over the next 75 years. One of its most impressive features, however, was added in 1881: the dining room by the architectural firm Mead, White, and McKim, a breathtaking hall with a cork ceiling and what is believed to be the earliest-ever installation of Tiffany stained glass windows, that manages to be grand and intimate at the same time.

Next door, Mead, White, and McKim went on to build the Isaac Bell House (Bellevue Ave., 401/847-1000, www.newportmansions.org, 10 A.M.–4:30 P.M. daily late June–early Sept., $14 adults, $5 children 6–17, children under 6 free), a demonstrably less imposing residence that nevertheless ranks among the nation's most impressive examples of shingle-style architecture. Completed in 1883, it is a quirky house even by Newport standards, with bamboo-style porch columns and an open floor plan inspired by the grand houses of Japan. Three narrow brick chimneys rise from the many-gabled roofline. A single ticket is good for both Kingscote and the Isaac Bell House.

## The Elms

The first real eruption of grandeur on Bellevue Avenue is also one of the most appealing of Newport's mansions. The Elms (424 Bellevue Ave., 401/847-1000, www.newportmansions.org, 10 A.M.–5 P.M. daily early Apr.–mid-June, 10 A.M.–6 P.M. daily mid-June–early Sept., 10 A.M.–5 P.M. daily early Sept.–late Nov., 10 A.M.–4 P.M. daily late Nov.–Dec., $14 adults, $5 children 6–17, children under 6 free) is a near-perfect copy of an 18th-century French château, built for coal tycoon Edward J. Berwind in 1901. The grounds comprise 10 acres of landscaped parkland containing about 40 species of trees, plus dignified marble statuary and perfectly groomed shrubs. The interior, almost cozy compared to some mansions,

## TOURING THE MANSIONS

Boasting over 15 historic properties and 80 acres of gardens and parks, Newport's collection of sprawling mansions can seem an overwhelming tour indeed. If you're intent on seeing as much of them as possible, consider the following tips.

Buy tickets ahead of time. The crowds in high season can be crushing, so take advantage of some of the online packages available through the **Preservation Society of Newport County** (424 Bellevue Ave., 401/847-1000, www.newportmansions.org), which manages most of the major mansions (one exception is Belcourt Castle). While individual mansions can be pricey, the fees for combination tickets can be quite economical. For example, a ticket to The Breakers is $19 for adults ($5 children 6-17); however, The Breakers and one other mansion is $24 ($5 children). If you are a mansion freak, a ticket to see any five mansions is only $31 ($10 children). So try to gauge your interest in the mansions realistically beforehand to benefit from these savings.

Tours are offered quite regularly at the largest mansions (approximately every 15 minutes during high season and every 30 minutes in spring). Times vary at many of the smaller mansions, but generally the wait time is no longer than 30 minutes. And because most tours are finished in under an hour and the mansions are within easy walking distance of one another (and transportation is provided in the form of natural-gas trolleys between the houses), it is quite reasonable to plan three mansion tours in one day. Some ambitious visitors opt to do four or five, but it should be noted that there are only so many gilded ceilings and marble hallways the human eye can gaze upon before they all start to blend together. To fully appreciate the level of grandeur and detail, it may be wisest to take in three tours per day, leaving time for a change of scenery—Newport's beaches, downtown, or parks. If you've got children, of course, you'll need to reduce that further to one or two mansions at most. (A good alternative, included in the combination ticket, is a tour of the Green Animals Topiary Garden in Portsmouth.)

Finally, take the time to invest in a good map or guide. The society produces probably the best map to the Cliff Walk and Bellevue Avenue, which includes a level of detail down to each individual building in the area, color-coded by type (private home, house museum, university building), along with step-by-step information about the Cliff Walk and the locations of bus and trolley stops. Many other publishers and organizations produce their own maps and guides to the area; they are readily available at local book shops and convenience stores.

The mansions are wheelchair accessible; baby strollers are not allowed, however.

---

abounds with gadgets as The Elms was among the earliest Newport homes to be lighted and run by electricity. Tours are self-guided with digital audio players, a format that allows you to walk through the house in 30–90 minutes, depending on how many specific topics you choose to hear about.

As sumptuous and stunning as the Venetian-style dining room, the grand ballroom, and the airy conservatory are, The Elms's most fascinating rooms are the service quarters and working areas. You'll have the chance to tour the incredibly well-organized kitchen and pantry, the laundry room, a coal tunnel, and the boiler room that heated the mansion. If this aspect of mansion life really interests you, consider taking one of The Elms's Behind-the-Scenes guided tours ($15 pp), which give a particularly detailed sense of the inner workings of the mansion told from the perspective of the 40 women and men who groomed the grounds, cleaned the rooms, and prepared the meals. It's recommended that you book Behind-the-Scenes tours at least 24 hours in advance, as space is limited.

### Chepstow

Just north of the Salve Regina campus on

Narragansett Avenue, Chepstow (401/847-1000, www.newportmansions.org, 10 A.M.–4:30 P.M. daily late June–early Sept., $14 adults, $5 children 6–17, children under 6 free) is another early Newport mansion. An Italianate villa designed by George Champlin Mason and completed in 1860, its exterior is harmonious if less grand than some of its cousins. The esteemed collection of Hudson River School paintings, however, is worth the price of admission. A descendant of Lewis Morris, a signatory of the Declaration of Independence, owned this cottage.

## Château-sur-Mer

Continuing the taste for all things French following the Civil War, Château-sur-Mer (Bellevue Ave., 401/847-1000, www.newportmansions.org, 10 A.M.–5 P.M. daily early Apr.–mid-June, 10 A.M.–6 P.M. daily mid-June–early Sept., 10 A.M.–5 P.M. daily early Sept.–late Nov., 10 A.M.–4 P.M. daily late Nov.–Dec., $14 adults, $5 children 6–17, children under 6 free) might be considered the missing link between the large homes such as Kingscote and Chepstow and the true mansions like The Breakers and Rosecliff. It was first built in a blocky château style in 1852 for merchant and Far East importer William S. Wetmore. After he died, however, his children decided the home needed a makeover, commissioning architect Richard Morris Hunt to update it to a more modern style. Hunt transformed both interior and exterior into a grand ensemble of the most fashionable European designs. Before those pesky Vanderbilts moved to Newport in the 1890s, this massive home was the largest residence in Newport. The interior impresses immediately with a stairway out of *Gone with the Wind* and a morning room demonstrating intricate woodwork. Behind the house you can stroll through a colonial revival garden pavilion and a Victorian-inspired park with century-old copper beech trees and weeping willows.

## ◖ The Breakers

Each of Newport's mansions is an

The Breakers is the most sumptuous of Newport's mansions.

undeniably overwhelming display of wealth, beauty, and design, but even among such over-the-top grandeur, the most lavish of them all is The Breakers (44 Ochre Point Ave., 401/847-1000, www.newportmansions.org, 9 A.M.–5 P.M. daily Apr.–late June, 9 A.M.–6 P.M. daily late June–early Sept., 9 A.M.–5 P.M. daily early Sept.–Nov., 9 A.M.–4 P.M. daily late Nov.–Dec., $19 adults, $10 children 6–17, children under 6 free), completed in 1895 as the summer home of steamship and railroad giant Commodore Cornelius Vanderbilt II, the first among equals of "the 400," the nickname for the elite New York social circle that ran the country back in the day. Designed by an international dream team of architects, the house has no less than 70 rooms and is a dead ringer for Italy's most opulent 16th-century palazzos. Alas, Vanderbilt only enjoyed one summer of good health here—after a stroke in 1896, he died a few years later in 1899.

His children, however, more than enjoyed the estate, including the impressive 13-acre grounds, which overlook Cliff Walk and the Atlantic Ocean—it was the sound of the waves smashing against the rocks below that gave The Breakers its name. Inside, rooms are constructed with ample amounts of semi-precious stones, rare marble, baccarat crystal chandeliers, and even platinum leaf on the walls (platinum is the rarest and most expensive metal in the world for its ability not to tarnish). In the bathrooms, four faucets provide both hot and cold freshwater and saltwater, and the marble baths were so thick that servants had to fill and drain them several times with hot water before they'd hold enough heat. Then there is the 45-foot-high Great Hall, as grandiose a room as there ever was and the site of countless soirees during The Breakers's heyday. At some of them, it's said, guests slid down the polished banister on dining trays.

As at The Elms, the tour here is with an audio recording that is exceptionally well put together, allowing guests to journey through the house at their own pace—taking in a little or a lot of the detail along the way, or skipping rooms entirely if time is limited. As engaging as the audio tour may be, however, be sure to take the headphones off once or twice. It's easy to get into a herd mentality of drifting from one numbered station to another without properly taking in the scene around you. Touch the cold marble pillars, gaze up at the mosaics on the ceilings, and try to imagine what it must have been like to live surrounded by such wealth and opulence.

Before you leave, be sure to check out the **Breakers Stable** (Coggeshall Ave. and Bateman Ave.), designed by Richard Morris Hunt. It contains a collection of road coaches and other memorabilia from the Vanderbilt clan. It's a block west of Bellevue Avenue by way of Ruggles Avenue.

## Rosecliff

More French influence is evident down the street at Rosecliff (548 Bellevue Ave., 401/847-1000, www.newportmansions.org, 10 A.M.–5 P.M. daily early Apr.–mid-June, 10 A.M.–6 P.M. daily mid-June–early Sept., 10 A.M.–5 P.M. daily early Sept.–late Nov., 10 A.M.–4 P.M. daily late Nov.–Dec., $14 adults, $5 children 6–17, children under 6 free), built by Stanford White in 1902 and inspired by the Grand Trianon section of the palace at Versailles, France. Originally commissioned by Theresa and Hermann Oelrichs, it has been featured in a handful of movies, including *The Great Gatsby* and *Amistad*.

As her husband increasingly preferred the more laid-back social life out West, the home became more and more the domain of "Tessie" Fair Oelrichs, a colorful silver heiress from Nevada who became the center of Newport society for many years. Luckily, Oelrichs knew how to throw a fete, and the house is remembered for having hosted a magic-themed party at which Harry Houdini entertained the guests, as well as many other outlandish events. A tour highlight is walking through the largest ballroom in Newport (and that's saying a lot in this city).

Rosecliff's opulent exterior

If the rest of the home lacks the luster of Newport's grandest mansions, it's because many of the opulent furnishings from Oelrichs' day have been removed, giving some of the rooms a bit of an empty feeling. The colorful story of its mistress, however, more than makes up for it. Sadly, she subsequently experienced a complete mental breakdown, living in seclusion for several years before her death in 1926, supposedly reliving her storied parties with imaginary guests.

## Astors' Beechwood Mansion

While none of the bigger and best-known mansions in the area are still owned by their original families, for many years one of them almost seemed to be: Astors' Beechwood (580 Bellevue Ave.) was long home to the Beechwood Theatre Company, which gave tours portraying the Astors, their friends, and their staff at the height of the Victorian era, becoming a steady favorite on the "cottage circuit." Alas, the mansion was sold for upward of $10 million in 2010, and the theater company disbanded. The current plans for the mansion are still under wraps, but it seems it will no longer be open for tours, a shame given its place in Newport Gilded Age society. The facade of the building can still be admired from the outside.

When William Backhouse Astor Jr. purchased a modest summer cottage in 1881, he hired architect Richard Morris Hunt to do a complete renovation along the lines of an Italianate summer villa. It was his wife, Caroline Astor, who ran the house as well as most of Newport Society. Known as "The Mrs. Astor," she virtually created the exclusive New York social circle known as "the 400" and held court with an austere presence for the two months of the year she summered at Newport—culminating every year in her famous Summer Ball.

## Marble House and Belcourt Castle

Another modest little Vanderbilt home is Marble House (596 Bellevue Ave., 401/847-1000, www.newportmansions.org, 10 A.M.–5 P.M. daily early Apr.–mid-June,

10 A.M.–6 P.M. daily mid-June–early Sept., 10 A.M.–5 P.M. daily early Sept.–late Nov., 10 A.M.–4 P.M. daily late Nov.–Dec., $14 adults, $5 children 6–17, children under 6 free), built in 1892 by Richard Morris Hunt for Cornelius Vanderbilt's grandson once removed, William K. Vanderbilt, who commissioned the home as a present for his wife, Alva, for her 39th birthday (which makes you wonder what he gave her for her 40th). True to its name, it's now filled with nearly half a million cubic feet of marble and includes on its grounds a Chinese teahouse built by Alva overlooking the crashing waves of the Atlantic below. After The Breakers, this is one of Newport's most-visited house-museums—visitors can't seem to get enough of the stairwells, columns, and floors of Italian, American, and African marble.

You'll find about 2,000 works of art—paintings, sculptures, and antiquities—at Belcourt Castle (657 Bellevue Ave., 401/846-0669, www.belcourtcastle.com, regular tours noon–5 P.M. daily May–Oct., weekends Apr. and Nov., closed Dec.–Mar., specialty tours available at other times, $20 adults, $16 youth under 17 and seniors). This Louis XIII–style castle hosts afternoon teas and many special events. The home was built by the rather idiosyncratic Oliver Hazard Perry Belmont, who inherited untold millions as the heir to the Rothschild fortune. Built in 1894 by, you guessed it, Richard Morris Hunt, the 60-room cottage cost $3 million. Belmont kept a staff of about 40 servants and owned an ornate collection of rare armor, manuscripts, and art from more than 30 Asian and European nations.

Now on regular guided tours you can examine the mansion's superb collection of French antiquities and art, most pieces dating from Louis XI through the Napoleonic periods. Tours cover not only the history of Belcourt but also that of several European royal castles, some of whose treasures now adorn this grand mansion. Belcourt also has the inevitable ghosts, and you can learn more about them during the Wednesday and Thursday ghost tours. Unlike most Newport mansions, Belcourt isn't run by the Preservation Society of Newport County, so a separate admission applies.

## ◖ CLIFF WALK

The two finest things Newport has to offer—its natural seaside beauty and the architectural relics of the Gilded Age—collide along the seaside Cliff Walk (www.cliffwalk.com), arguably one of the country's grandest strolls. Beginning at the western end of First Beach (also known as Easton's Beach), the 3.5-mile path runs between the rocky beach and many of the town's most impressive mansions. The area is a designated National Historic District and was deemed a National Recreational Trail in 1975, making it a double-whammy of natural and artificial glory. For many who walk it, the Cliff Walk is an opportunity to gaze at fancy estates and experience the same ocean views that mesmerized Newport's wealthy summer visitors at the turn of the 20th century. It is also a wonderful nature trail, abundant with opportunities for bird-watching and for admiring fields of wildflowers.

There are a number of access points along Cliff Walk, but none are near ample public parking except the beginning of the trail at Easton's Beach, so the other points are limited to pedestrians and cyclists. Sheppard Avenue, Webster Street, and Wetmore Avenue intersect the walk about midway and have some limited street parking, and Narragansett Avenue, about 0.5 miles into the walk, has the most parking of any intersecting streets. During the summer a bus runs up and down Bellevue Avenue, the main paved road that parallels the walk, and you can take the bus to any of the cross streets that lead to the walk.

Less than a mile into the walk, at the end of Narragansett Avenue, you'll come to the **40 Steps,** a sharply descending stone stairway that goes nearly to the sea below; from a small promontory at the base of the steps you can watch the waves smashing against the rocks.

Newport's dramatic Cliff Walk

Soon after 40 Steps, the path meanders by some of Newport's most famous mansions, including The Breakers, Rosecliff, Astor's Beechwood, and Marble House. Soon after, on the right and just above the path, you'll see the ornate red Chinese teahouse commissioned by Marble House's owner, Alva Vanderbilt. At this point the Cliff Walk cuts through a short tunnel before emerging again for another fairly well maintained stretch and then a second tunnel.

Once you emerge from this final tunnel, Cliff Walk becomes a scramble on the wild side, as it hugs the rocky shoreline by a series of large private homes. This span is aptly nicknamed **Rough Point,** and rather crude and ugly chain-link fences separate the path from the private properties. Northeasters and hurricanes have taken their toll on Cliff Walk's southern reaches, and in some places the seawall has been ripped out. It's all entirely passable, and it's generally not too steep or high, but you do want to wear sturdy shoes. As you cut around the southeastern tip of the peninsula, you'll be able to see the Doris Duke estate, Rough Point, just off Bellevue where it bends from south to west.

As Cliff Walk turns west around the southeastern tip of Newport, you'll come to Ledge Road, a short dead-end that shoots south off Bellevue Avenue. At this point you might think that Cliff Walk comes to an end—indeed, a short walk up Ledge Road does lead you back to where buses pass along Bellevue Avenue. However, it's also entirely possible to climb along the jagged rocks, treading carefully, for a short distance around the southwestern tip of this small peninsula. After a little more than 0.25 miles of cutting your own trail, the official Cliff Walk resumes, now in a northerly direction along the western end of the peninsula. To your left, looking northwest, you'll see the exclusive **Bailey's Beach,** and before long you'll reach the eastern edge of this fabled stretch of sand.

For a detailed sense of the entire walk's

history and highlights, the official website (www.cliffwalk.com) has detailed maps and 360-degree panoramas of some of the most beautiful spots along the trail.

## MIDDLETOWN

Part of Newport until 1743, Middletown (population 17,000) is a relatively sleepy town. There isn't a lot to do here except relax and admire the area's pristine beaches, historic homes, and natural scenery. If that's your idea of an ideal sojourn, you've come to the right place.

Like Newport, Middletown suffered at the hands of the Brits during the Revolutionary War. A fleet of 11 British ships landed in Middletown in December 1776 to begin their occupation of lower Aquidneck Island. They are said to have looted many private homes, and more than a quarter of the community's residents fled to the mainland.

These days, most visitors make their way here from Newport for the day for one of the beaches or bird-watching at the local bird sanctuary, or to take advantage of cheaper accommodations while touring Newport.

### Sights

The Newport-Middletown border lies on the eastern end of Easton's Beach, otherwise known as First Beach. From there, Memorial Boulevard becomes Purgatory Road, passing by the campus of **St. George's School** (off Purgatory Road), a private seminary for boys that was founded in 1896. After passing St. George's, you can reach Second Beach by bearing left onto Paradise Road and then quickly right onto Hanging Rocks Road—you'll see parking on the right.

The parking lot nearest Newport at Second Beach is a short walk from **Purgatory Chasm,** a 160-foot-deep fissure in the cliffs that ranges 8–15 feet in width at the top and 2–20 feet at the bottom. There's a small parking area (maximum 30 minutes) at the short trail to the chasm itself. This narrow and perhaps overhyped geological feature, with a nice little wooden bridge over it, has been a curiosity for as long as anybody can remember. Still, it's fun to sit on the rocky promontory and admire the view down over Second Beach. Second Beach also has a small campground that occupies an enviable spot between Sachuest Point and Gardiners Pond; camping facilities include RV hookups and restrooms.

From here, continue east along Sachuest Road to reach **Sachuest Point National Wildlife Refuge** (Sachuest Point Rd.), which has a visitors center that's good for trail maps and local information. The center sits on a small bluff that affords nice views back toward Newport. Looking up the hill to the north of Newport, you'll also see the Gothic towers of St. George's prep school. Anglers appreciate the miles of rocky shoreline; the preserve also has some good hiking.

Backtrack along Sachuest Road past Gardiners Pond, make a right onto Indian Avenue, and follow it to Third Beach Road, which leads to—you guessed it—**Third Beach.** A short distance up the hill along Third Beach Road is the entrance to the **Norman Bird Sanctuary** (583 Third Beach Rd., 401/846-2577, www.normanbirdsanctuary.org, 9 A.M.–5 P.M. daily, $6), which occupies a small hill overlooking Second and Third Beaches, Sachuest Point, and the ocean. The refuge encompasses over 300 acres of farm fields, meadows, woodlands, and rocky ridges. In addition to hiking trails, the sanctuary boasts a small museum inside a historic barn, with exhibits about beach ecology and Native American history as well as live snakes, rodents, and raptors found on the sanctuary. Various educational walks and programs geared toward experts and novices, adults and families are offered throughout the year. During the spring and fall migrations, bird walks are held at 8 A.M. Sunday. If you don't have a car, you can still get to the sanctuary during the summer months by taking the **Coyote Shuttle** ($5 round-trip), a bus that leaves from the Newport Gateway Visitors Center hourly to make the rounds of several Middletown attractions.

If you bear left after Second Beach instead

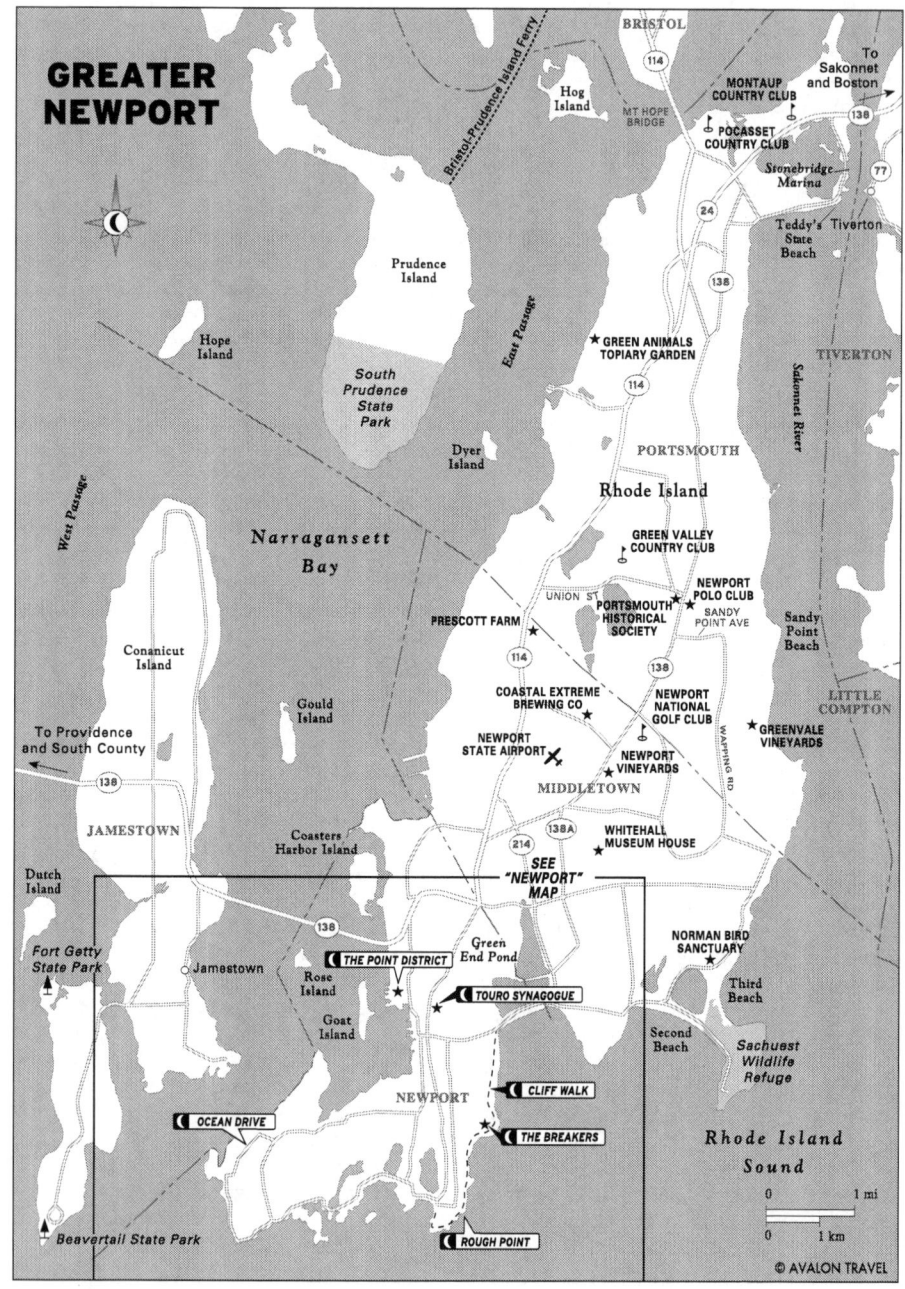

of bearing right toward Third Beach, you'll hit Indian Avenue, a rolling road lined with handsome, mostly early-20th-century homes that fringes the Sakonnet River. It's a beautiful stretch that's less fancy but also much less pretentious than Ocean Drive and Bellevue Avenue. Indian Avenue runs for about 2.5 miles before dead-ending; shortly before it ends, you can make a left turn onto Old Mill Lane and follow it a short way to Wapping Road, the main north-south route on Aquidneck Island.

From where Old Mill Lane intersects with Wapping Road, it's roughly one mile until you reach the right-hand turnoff for **Greenvale Vineyards** (582 Wapping Rd., 401/847-3777, www.greenvale.com, 10 A.M.–5 P.M. Mon.–Sat., noon–5 P.M. Sun.). Tastings at this attractive winery are held in a distinctive old gray building with a mansard roof. The breezes from the Sakonnet River keep things pretty cool even on hot summer days, making it a nice excursion in July and August. Back on Wapping Road, you can head north another mile or so until the road runs into Sandy Point Avenue; here a right turn leads down the hill to **Sandy Point Beach**, along the western shores of the Sakonnet River. This scenic beach is broad and flat and ideal for a picnic. In the other direction, Sandy Point Avenue runs west for about 0.5 miles until hitting East Main Road (Route 138).

Middletown may not have a Main Street, but it has two Main Roads—an East one and a West one, which run roughly parallel up the island from Newport. Both are accessible from downtown Newport by heading north on Marlborough Street from the Marriott, then north on Broadway from Washington Square. (Route 138 can also be reached by heading directly north up Memorial Blvd.)

Both routes also have attractions worth visiting. On West Main Road, a mile north from the intersection with Union Street, is the turn-off for Newport Restoration Society's third main property, **Prescott Farm** (2009 W. Main Rd., Middletown, 401/849-7300, www.newportrestoration.com, dawn–dusk daily year-round, free). This 40-acre farmstead, purchased by doyenne Doris Duke to preserve Aquidneck's farming history, makes an engaging alternative to the crowded mansions of Newport as well as a fascinating look at agrarian culture during Newport's colonial times. Among the attractions here is a 1730s guardhouse that contains notable Early American furnishings from the 17th century and an original 1812 windmill, still used today to grind grain, that spent time on several farms in the area after it was first built and installed in Warren.

Between West and East Main Streets is Newport State Airport; just north of it, take a turn onto Oliphant Avenue, one mile south of Prescott Farm or four miles north of downtown Newport, to find Rhode Island's only true microbrewery, **Coastal Extreme Brewing Co.** (307 Oliphant Lane, Middletown, 401/849-5232, www.newportstorm.com, noon–5 P.M. Wed.–Mon.), maker of the popular Newport Storm line of beers. In addition to its flagship Hurricane Amber Ale, the brewery produces Regenschauer Oktoberfest (available only in the fall), Blizzard Porter, Thunderhead Irish Red, and Maelstrom IPA. The visitors center is open every afternoon except Tuesday, and tours ($7), which include samples of several beers as well as a souvenir crystal beer glass, are given when there are enough visitors.

If you are still thirsty, the second of the area's wineries, **Newport Vineyards** (909 E. Main Rd., Rte. 138, Middletown, 401/848-5161, www.newportvineyards.com, 10 A.M.–5 P.M. Mon.–Sat., noon–5 P.M. Sun.), is a short drive away on East Main Street, just across from the airport. The winery produces several white and red varieties, including a riesling, a chardonnay, and a merlot, with tastings during opening hours and tours at 1 and 3 P.M. daily. As if that weren't enough, on the property you'll also find a toy store, a garden center, an art gallery, and a small restaurant; a farmers market is held on the grounds Saturday morning June–October.

Finally, 0.5 miles south of the winery just off Route 138, head east on Wyatt Road and south onto Berkeley Avenue by Middletown Cemetery to find an altogether different house-museum dedicated to noted Irish philosopher George Berkeley, who lived in Middletown 1729–1731 in the **Whitehall Museum House** (311 Berkeley Ave., 401/846-3116, http://whitehallmuseumhouse.org, 10 A.M.–4 P.M. Tues.–Sun., $5 adults, free for children under 15). It is a stately red saltbox that has been managed by the Rhode Island chapter of Colonial Dames since 1900 and is now furnished with period pieces (although none belonged to Berkeley himself). Berkeley was in Aquidneck on a 20,000-pound commission from the British parliament to found a college in Bermuda to educate the sons of colonists and Indians in the New World. A literary and ecclesiastical salon of sorts was begun here during Berkeley's time, and even though his commission fell through and he returned home after three years, he left behind the impetus for founding Brown and Columbia Universities. Later, when the University of California was looking for a name for a new town outside San Francisco where they were founding a school, they named it Berkeley in his honor.

# PORTSMOUTH

Rounding out the tip of Aquidneck Island, north of Middletown, the town of Portsmouth (population 17,000) tends to get missed by many visitors to Newport, even though it claims to be nothing less than the "birthplace of American democracy." While that might seem like municipal hubris, it's actually not far off the mark: Founded in 1638 by religious heretics banished from Massachusetts Bay, including feminist preacher Anne Hutchinson, the town was the first to be ruled by its own members instead of the crown of England. A bronze tablet erected on a rock at Founders Brook memorializes the so-called Portsmouth Compact that founded the independent community.

The town played a minor part in the Revolutionary War as the site of the Battle of Rhode Island, which took place in August 1778 as a group of American troops led by General John Sullivan ventured by boat from Tiverton to Portsmouth, where they drove British forces back nearly to Newport. After the Revolutionary War, Portsmouth's early economy involved two things that Aquidneck Island has long excelled in: farming and shipbuilding. Unusually in this part of the country, the town also did quite well with coal mining for a time—a large coal field on the western side of town produced large quantities of coal. Portsmouth today has its own rather modest summer colony, mostly along or just off Route 138, which runs down the eastern side of the town overlooking the Sakonnet River.

## Sights

As with Middletown, Portsmouth attractions are divided between West and East Main Road. You can learn more about Portsmouth's impressive early history at the **Portsmouth Historical Society** (870 E. Main Rd., Rte. 138 at Union St., 401/683-9178, limited hours), which occupies the town's former Christian Union Church (circa 1865), 0.5 miles north of Sandy Point Avenue. Also on the grounds are the 1845 Portsmouth Town Hall and the Southernmost School, Rhode Island's oldest one-room schoolhouse, which dates to 1725.

From here it's a rather long but pleasant journey north on Route 138, which passes modern shopping centers along the way but is generally an appealing thoroughfare with several good views out over the Sakonnet River and toward the Sakonnet Peninsula. After about 4.5 miles, Route 138 bears right and becomes Park Avenue, which leads to an interesting, rather modest beach community called Island Park. Where Route 138 abruptly shifts to the left, stay on Park Avenue and continue straight for another mile to the Stonebridge Marina, on the right. You'll pass some fun little seafood eateries, the most famous being Flo's Clam Shack.

The marina marks the spot where a stone bridge across the Sakonnet River once connected Portsmouth to Tiverton, but the bridge was removed in 1956, leaving fishing piers on both shores—it's less than 200 yards between the ends of the piers. There's also a nice sandy beach by the marina. To the north, in the immediate distance, you'll see the massive new highway bridge, where Route 138/24 runs between Portsmouth and Tiverton.

From Stonebridge Marina, drive about 0.5 mile north and under the Route 138 overpass, making a left turn onto Hummocks Avenue. Follow it a short way south until it becomes Anthony Road; you're paralleling Route 138/24, which is on your left. When you reach Boyds Lane, turn right and head into the small village of Bristol Ferry, where a boat used to carry passengers across Narragansett Bay to the southern tip of Bristol. In 1927 the Mount Hope Bridge was constructed, carrying traffic along Route 114 across the bay. It is a narrow, graceful bridge, and from the top of its arch you'll enjoy great views out over the bay and Aquidneck Island.

From here, you can turn around and retrace your route back south along Route 114. Three miles south, turn right on Cory's Lane to arrive at the **Green Animals Topiary Garden** (380 Cory's Lane, 401/847-1000, www.newportmansions.org, 10 A.M.–6 P.M. daily Apr.–mid-Oct., $12 adults, $4.50 children 6–17), where humanity and shrubbery peacefully coexist in a menagerie of some 80 shrubs and trees sculpted into whimsical shapes, some of which have been intriguing visitors for almost a century. Among them are teddy bears, a giraffe, a unicorn, and an elephant. Also on the grounds is a small museum of Victorian toys, and there's an extensive gift shop of toys, garden items, and the like. Green Animals admission is included with the combination ticket for Hunter House and several Bellevue Avenue mansions.

## JAMESTOWN

In the middle of Narragansett Bay between Newport and South County, the town of Jamestown occupies all of Conanicut Island, a cigar-shaped swatch of land with a smaller island off its southwestern tip. With a full-time population of 6,000, the island is not at all densely populated, although improved bridges have been built in recent decades and southern Rhode Island has expanded in general, making Jamestown a full-time home for more people.

It's a lovely island to explore, and Jamestown's tiny but picturesque downtown has several cute shops and a handful of notable eateries and accommodations. The leading attraction is the tremendous scenic beauty, and **Beavertail State Park** (Beavertail Rd., 401/423-9941 or 401/884-2010, www.riparks.com) covers 155 acres of pristine scrub and low woodland across a rocky point at the southern end of Conanicut Island. A loop road runs through much of the park and passes several scenic overlooks, including one that takes in Beavertail Lighthouse. The park is laced with hiking trails, and throughout the summer park naturalists lead a variety of walks.

# Entertainment and Events

## ARTS AND CULTURE

Considering Newport's glittering legacy of sophisticated and wealthy summer visitors along with its well-endowed visual arts scene, the city is relatively lacking when it comes to the performing arts.

One of the most popular entertainment venues is the **Newport Playhouse and Cabaret Restaurant** (102 Connell Hwy., near the foot of Newport Bridge, 401/848-PLAY—401/848-7529, www.newportplayhouse.com), which presents several generally light theatrical performances each year April–December. The show comes with a substantial buffet dinner, and the theater has a full liquor license. Different kinds of music concerts are sometimes held at the city's house-museums, churches, and at Salve Regina University's **Cecilia Hall** (in the Carey Mansion, Ruggles Ave., 401/341-2945). It's best to check with the **Newport County Convention and Visitors Bureau** (23 America's Cup Ave., next to the bus terminal, Newport, 401/849-8098 or 800/326-6030, www.gonewport.com) for details on what's happening where.

## NIGHTLIFE

For a city of just 26,000, Newport does pack quite a punch when it comes to nightlife.

There's often live music at **Christie's** (351 Thames St., 401/847-5400), a fun gathering spot for schmoozing; the crowd tends to look as if they were fresh out of a J. Crew catalog. Below the Candy Store at Bannister's Wharf, the **Boom Boom Room** (1 Bannister's Wharf, 401/849-2900) draws a fairly mainstream and somewhat touristy crowd for dancing to DJ-spun Top 40 and disco hits. Upstairs in the bar at **Candy Store** (401/849-2900), yachting enthusiasts and Newport socialites trade gossip and cruise over wines by the glass and fancy cocktails. **Sabina Doyle's** (359 Thames St., 401/849-4466, http://fastour.com/sabina/) is a more centrally located Irish pub that's also quite fun. Over near the beaches, summer vacationers often congregate at **KJ's Pub** (61 Aquidneck Ave., 401/848-9991, http://kjsrestaurant.com), which serves decent seafood and burgers and often books live acoustic, blues, and other music.

Sing-alongs are a favorite pastime at the piano bar at **La Forge Casino Restaurant** (186 Bellevue Ave., 401/847-0418), which gets going on Friday and Saturday evenings. It tends to be a less chaotic alternative to the sometimes rowdy collegiate bars down along Thames Street. **Vincent's on the Pier** (10 W. Howard's Wharf, 401/847-3645, www.vincentsonthepier.com) presents very nice piano music, and nearly every table in this restaurant-bar overlooks Newport Harbor. The kitchen (lunch noon–3 P.M. daily, dinner 6–9:30 P.M. Sun.–Thurs., 6–10 P.M. Fri.–Sat.) turns out first-rate, upscale Mediterranean and new American cuisine. **Castaway's on Solar Wind** (28 Prospect Hill St., 401/849-9928) is Newport's small but festive gay nightspot, noted for its vintage antique bar. It's a classy little spot with a nice side bar that has a pool table.

### Live Music and Clubs

Jazz lovers who couldn't be in town for the Newport Jazz Festival or just want a second show will find proper consolation at the **Newport Blues Cafe** (286 Thames St., 401/841-5510, www.newportblues.com). The restaurant-lounge showcases live music from acclaimed artists seven nights a week. Progressive rock fans can catch indie acts—some big names, but mostly local—at **One Pelham East** (270 Thames St., 401/847-9460, www.thepelham.com). Usually packed on summer nights, it can be a comfortable spot to catch fall and winter acts.

The **Rhino Bar and Grille** (337 Thames St., 401/846-0707, www.therhinobar.com) is a mainstay for listening to live bands and dancing to DJ-spun techno, hip-hop, and dance tunes. The crowd is young and cruisy, generally on the make, and looking to have a good time. The grill serves better-than-average American food, pizzas, burgers, and grills, and there is a surprisingly sophisticated wine list.

## FESTIVALS AND EVENTS
### Summer

In early June, the **Schweppes Great Chowder Cook-off** (www.newportfestivals.com) is great fun. You can get a neat behind-the-fence look at many Newport properties on the **Secret Garden Tour** (www.secretgardentour.com), held in early June and then again in September.

Also in early June, look for the **Newport International Film Festival** (www.newportfilmfestival.com), a prestigious six-day festival of dozens of films that include features, special screenings, documentaries, and numerous shorts; there's usually a retrospective each year too. Many lectures, parties, and other events coincide with the film festival. At Rosecliff, the **Newport Flower Show** (www.newportmansions.org) is held at the end of June, filling tents with exotic plants and flower arrangements organized around a different theme each year. The **Snapple Sunset Music Festival** (www.newportfestivals.com), in late June–early July, brings national folk and rock acts to an intimate waterfront venue.

Newport's **Portuguese Cultural Festival** is held in early July in Touro Park, and features traditional Portuguese food along with music and folk dancing. A variety of venues hosts the **Newport Music Festival** (www.newportmusic.org), which has been going strong since the late 1960s. The event runs for roughly

## NEWPORT JAZZ FESTIVAL

Every August, Newport's already impressive number of summer visitors swells by leaps and bounds thanks to one thing: the global draw of the renowned Newport Jazz Festival. Founded as the first outdoor jazz music festival by pianist George Wein and several Newport socialites in 1954, the festival is now a magnet for jazz fans for its mix of well-known performers and up-and-coming musicians. Over the decades, legends like Miles Davis, Duke Ellington, Billie Holiday, and Frank Sinatra have graced its stages.

Usually a three-day series of concerts and events, the festival packs in hundreds of performances, from organ trios and vocalists to Brazilian duos and big-band productions, on three primary stages. Performance schedules are always available ahead of time from the festival office (401/847-3700, www.jazzfestival55.com). Tickets are plentiful and can be bought in advance and by showing up in person. Regulars strongly recommend booking a hotel ahead of time, as the more desirable properties book up months in advance. There is also camping offered nearby in Melville Ponds Campground (401/682-2424) in Portsmouth.

Most of the festival's action takes place in Fort Adams State Park on Harrison Avenue, which has strict rules about what attendees may bring. When packing, bear in mind that they allow only one small handheld cooler per person; individual blankets must measure less than 8 by 10 feet; and only low-backed chairs (under 30 inches) are allowed, to ensure good viewing for those around you. No glass containers, alcohol, pets, bikes, or beach umbrellas are permitted. Children are welcome, and there are plenty of inexpensive kids' meals at the concession stands.

---

the last two weeks of July and presents about 60 chamber-music and other classical concerts at some of the city's most famous mansions, including The Elms, The Breakers, Marble House, Salve Regina's Ochre Court, Rosecliff, and Belcourt Castle. Some of the concerts are held in ballrooms and indoor spaces, while others are presented under tent cover on the lush grounds. The **Newport Summer Comedy Series** (Newport Yachting Center, America's Cup Ave., www.newportcomedy.com) runs July–August and consists of a series of comedy shows held every Sunday night. The sponsors book mostly New England–based comedians, including several who have performed on late-night talk shows and have received awards at the prestigious Boston Comedy Festival.

Also in early July is the **Newport Kite Festival** (www.buyakite.com), with kite flying shows and demonstrations open to the public free of charge. Toward the end of the July the **Black Ships Festival** (401/847-7666, www.blackshipsfestival.com) celebrates the 1854 opening of U.S. trade with Japan by Newport's Commodore Matthew Perry. It is a citywide celebration of his trip and of Japanese culture. The International Tennis Hall of Fame hosts the **Campbell's Hall of Fame Tennis Championship** (www.tennisfame.org), a major draw on the Association of Tennis Professionals tour and the only grass-court professional tennis tourney in the country.

More music enjoyment is to be had at the **Apple and Eve Newport Folk Festival** (www.newportfolk.com). This three-day event, held at the sprawling, well-kept Fort Adams State Park in early August, is one of the nation's top folk festivals and has drawn dozens of major artists through the years; recent performers include Bob Dylan, Shawn Colvin, Arlo Guthrie, Dar Williams, and Bruce Cockburn. The following weekend in August, the hugely popular **Newport Jazz Festival** (401/848-5055, www.jazzfestival55.com) is also held at Fort Adams. Big international acts congregate here alongside promising up-and-comers to entertain jazz enthusiasts.

## Fall

Over Labor Day weekend, the **Classic Yacht**

**Regatta and Parade Day** (www.moy.org) features about 100 vintage sailing vessels racing on Narragansett Bay; there's also a parade of ships. Around the same time is the ever-growing annual **Newport Waterfront Irish Festival** (401/846-1600, www.newportwaterfrontevents.com), which brings step-dancing, bagpipes, and Guinness to the waterfront. The city's many avid yachters make a point of visiting the annual **Newport International Boat Show** (www.newportexhibition.com). Later in September you can attend the **Tastes of Rhode Island Festival** (www.newportwaterfrontevents.com) and sample dishes offered by the state's top chefs. **Haunted Newport** (401/845-9123, www.hauntednewport.com) is held the last week in October and includes tours of area houses set up for the ghoulish holiday.

In early October, check out the **Norman Bird Sanctuary Harvest Fair** (www.normanbirdsanctuary.org), a 2-day celebration of fall with children's games, hayrides, and craft vendors. The city's **Fiesta Italiana**, in mid-October, celebrates Newport's Italian heritage with food, music, storytelling, and other family-oriented events. Mid-October also features **International Oktoberfest** (www.newportwaterfrontevents.com), a traditional Bavarian festival with wurst and oompah bands, as well as the **Bowen's Wharf Seafood Festival** (www.bowenswharf.com), which offers lobster, stuffies, scallops, oysters, and other tasty dishes from local restaurants and fishermen, along with live Celtic music, folk songs, and sea shanties.

## Winter and Spring

All through mid-November until Christmas, the holiday season sees the town's mansions decked out even more elaborately than usual; heavyweights such as Marble House and The Breakers are festively dressed in white lights and Christmas decorations for **Christmas at the Newport Mansions** (401/847-1000, www.newportmansions.org, late Nov.–early Jan., admission cost varies for different mansions). All through December is the annual **Christmas in Newport Celebration** (www.christmasinnewport.org), which fills the waterfront and historic

Newport's annual International Boat Show is a haven for yachters.

districts with thousands of white lights and Christmas music from live bands and choruses.

Newport tries hard to keep things lively through the colder months by throwing **12 Weeks of Winter** (www.gonewport.com) January–March. Each week has a different theme—popular ones include Cultural Arts Week; Mystery Week; Antiques and Collectibles Week; Black Heritage Week; the Kinsale, Ireland, Festival of Fine Food (Kinsale is Newport's sister city); and the Newport Winter Festival.

Come spring, every boat lover in New England heads for the **Spring Boat Show** (401/846-1115, www.newportspringboatshow.com, $5 adults, free for children under 12) in late May, the region's largest, to ogle the new and used vessels and to haggle at the stalls of the show's flea market, where everything from fishing line to used kayak paddles are for sale. Also in late May is the **Sail Newport Family Sailing Festival** (www.sailnewport.org), in which experienced sailors give free tours of the harbor, and **Fort Adams Day** (www.fortadams.org), which features kids' games, food, and tours of the fort.

## Shopping

Newport can keep even the most dedicated shoppers content for days. In the downtown area, along Thames Street and the lanes and wharves just off it, you'll find dozens of mostly independent clothiers, jewelry shops, art galleries, and gift shops. Chain businesses have made some inroads, but for the most part you'll find a nice mix of stores that you won't find back home or even in other parts of Rhode Island.

Most of the house-museums along Bellevue Avenue have outstanding gift shops, and the proceeds help to keep these mansions running. Books on local and regional architecture and decorative arts, prints, and housewares are among the most common items you'll find in these shops.

Another Newport retail specialty is decorative and practical wares with a nautical bent, from the requisite ship's wheel and scrimshaw kitsch to high-quality maritime paintings and prints, sailing clothing and gear, and antique barometers, ships' clocks, and similar items. Quite a few local artists live in or near Newport and have their creations represented at galleries around town.

### SHOPPING DISTRICTS

Several of the wharves in Newport function today as mini malls, many of them on the wharves jutting into the harbor. **Bannister's Wharf** (off Thames St., www.bannisterswharf.net) has several fine shops. **Brahmin Handbags** (22 Bannister's Wharf, 401/849-5990, 10 A.M.–8 P.M. daily) is where to find high-quality handmade leather accessories that include prim and classic New England handbags to funky wallets that would be at home on the Riviera. Looking for something to wear out to dinner tonight? Turn to **Mandarine** (16 Bannister's Wharf, 401/848-9360, www.shopmandarine.com, 10 A.M.–6 P.M. Mon.–Sat., 10 A.M.–5 P.M. Sun.), which carries smart men's and women's sportswear and cocktail party–worthy gear. Pick up silk dresses, jewelry, suits, and accessories by designers from all over the globe.

**Bowen's Wharf** (Thames St. at America's Cup Ave., 401/849-2243, www.bowenswharf.com, 10 A.M.–10 P.M. Mon.–Sat., noon–7 P.M. Sun.) is a bit smaller than Bannister's Wharf but has an engaging mix of businesses, including Crabtree & Evelyn, Thomas Kinkade Galleries, and about 20 other shops, plus several restaurants, harbor tour companies, and galleries. Highlights include **Bellevue Beauty Walk** (2 Bowen's Wharf, 401/845-0800, www.bellevuebeautywalk.com, 10 A.M.–9 P.M. Mon.–Sat., noon–6 P.M. Sun.)—which stocks marquee lines such as Molton Brown, Paula Dorf, and Terax hair care—and **Michael Hayes** (204 Bellevue Ave., 401/846-3090, www.michaelhayesnewport.com, 10 A.M.–10 P.M. daily) for topnotch women's lines like Missoni and Roberto Cavalli

shopping on Bowen's Wharf

along with men's duds by Ermenegildo Zegna and Etro. **Thames Glass** (688 Thames St., 401/846-0576, 10 A.M.–6 P.M. Mon.–Sat., noon–5 P.M. Sun.) carries the handblown glasswork of Newport artist Matthew Buechner; you can take glassblowing lessons here too.

## ARTS AND CRAFTS

There are many very good sources of nautical and marine art in town. One of the most extensive, **Arnold Art Store and Gallery** (210 Thames St., 401/847-2273, www.arnoldart.com, 9:30 A.M.–5:30 P.M. Mon.–Sat., noon–5 P.M. Sun.), fills three floors with original paintings and prints. Also highly acclaimed is **William Vareika Fine Arts** (212 Bellevue Ave., 401/849-6149, www.vareikafinearts.com, 10 A.M.–6 P.M. Mon.–Sat., 1–6 P.M. Sun., or by appointment), which carries exceptional American paintings, drawings, and watercolors from the past three centuries. **Blink Gallery** (89 Thames St., 401/847-4255, www.blinkgalleryusa.com, 10 A.M.–6 P.M. Mon.–Fri.) presents stunning contemporary photography with many scenes of Newport and other works depicting scenes from all over the world. **Onne Van Der Wal** (1 Bannister's Wharf, 401/846-5556, www.vanderwal.com, 10 A.M.–5 P.M. Mon.–Fri., 10 A.M.–6 P.M. Sat., noon–5 P.M. Sun., or by appointment) is another superb photography gallery and an excellent place to pick up a memento of Newport.

**Sheldon Fine Art** (59 America's Cup Ave., 401/849-0030, www.sheldonfineart.com, 9 A.M.–9 P.M. daily) carries the works of several prominent artists, including John Mecray and John Phillip Hagen. **Spring Bull Studio and Gallery** (55 Bellevue Ave., 401/849-9166, www.springbullgallery.com, noon–5 P.M. daily) is a cooperative gallery of nearly 20 area artists. Contemporary jewelry and decorative arts are the specialty at **Suydam and Diepenbrock** (9 Bridge St., 401/848-9090). At **Cadeaux du Monde** (26 Mary St., 401/848-0550, www.cadeauxdumonde.com), you can browse folk art, textiles, clothing, and decorative arts from around the world, especially Latin America. **Roger King Fine Arts** (21 Bowen's Wharf, 401/847-4359, www.rkingfinearts.com, 10 A.M.–5 P.M. daily) carries an impressive selection of 19th- and 20th-century paintings, especially nautically themed works.

## ANTIQUES, GIFTS, AND HOME FURNISHINGS

The **Griffon Shop** (76 Bellevue Ave., 401/848-8200, 10 A.M.–4 P.M. Tues.–Sat., 1–4 P.M. Sun.) carries a wide range of antiques, odds and ends, and original artwork by several local artists and craftspeople.

Another bric-a-brac emporium of solid repute is the **Eagle's Nest Antique Center** (3101 E. Main Rd., Rte. 138, Portsmouth, 401/683-3500, 11 A.M.–5 P.M. Mon.–Sat., noon–5 P.M. Sun.), a multiple-dealer space with more than 100 stalls representing every possible kind of antique, collectible, jewelry, and toy.

**Karen Vaughan** (148 Bellevue Ave., 401/848-2121, www.karenvaughanonline.com, 9 A.M.–5 P.M. Mon.–Fri.) carries a natty array of hip home furnishings and decorative arts. Furniture-maker Jeffrey Greene crafts fine 18th century–inspired designs at **The Ball and Claw** (55 America's Cup Ave., 401/848-5600, www.theballandclaw.com, 10:30 A.M.–6 P.M. Mon.–Thurs., 10:30 A.M.–7 P.M. Fri.–Sat., 11:30 A.M.–5:30 P.M. Sun.), which also carries porcelain, quilts, chandeliers, and lamps. For nearly a century, **J.T.'s Chandlery** (128 Spring St., 401/846-7256, www.jtschandlery.com, 10 A.M.–8 P.M. daily) has been a leading supplier of all things nautical; it's still a must for yachting and boating aficionados and a great source of gifts.

You can pick up reproduction home furnishings, gifts, and jewelry of Newport's Gilded Age at the **Museum Store** (Preservation Society of Newport, 1 Bannister's Wharf, 401/849-9900, www.newportmansions.org, 9 A.M.–10 P.M. daily. Before hitting the surf, hit the shelves and racks of **Helly Hansen** (154 Thames St., 877/666-8742, www.hellyengland.com, 9 A.M.–9 P.M. daily). The boating gear selection ranges from base layers to keep you warm on windy sails to fully waterproof parkas and snuggly soft shell jackets. Home to an excellent selection of stained-glass artwork, **Aardvark Antiques** (9 JT Connell Hwy., 401/849-7233, www.aardvarkantiques.com, 9 A.M.–5 P.M. Mon.–Sat., by appointment Sun.) is also where you'll find garden statues and fountains like nowhere else outside a Roman square: Giant gargoyles and ceramic fish squat next to structures festooned with mermaids and gods.

## PICK-YOUR-OWN FARMS

Pick-your-own farms are more popular in other parts of the state, but **Sweet Berry Farm** (19 Third Beach Rd., Middletown, 401/847-3912, www.sweetberryfarmri.com, 8 A.M.–7 P.M. daily) is a great spot for this activity within a short drive of downtown Newport. In summer, go for strawberries and raspberries, then move on to cut flowers and vegetables as the months progress, and finally find pumpkins in the fall and Christmas trees in early winter.

# Sports and Recreation

## FIRST, SECOND, AND THIRD BEACHES

Along with the mansions, day-trippers from all over New England come to Newport for shopping, boating, and especially sunbathing. Newport and neighboring Middletown have been blessed with several largely undeveloped stretches of golden sand that are some of the most beautiful on the Atlantic Coast. The beach starts in Newport near the Middletown border with Easton's Beach (175 Memorial Blvd., 401/845-5810, www.cityofnewport.com/departments/economic-development/beach/home.cfm)—otherwise known as First Beach, which curves between Easton's Pond and the Atlantic below the Cliff Walk. In addition to its picturesque setting, the beach is particularly good for families, with a bathhouse, a full restaurant, and lots of activities going on all the time.

Easton's Beach, also known as First Beach

Children's programs are held early on Thursday evenings, and other activities geared for kids take place daily at a miniature amusement park at the Easton's Beach Rotunda, which includes the popular **Easton's Beach Carousel** (10 A.M.–8 P.M. Sat.–Sun. late May–mid-June, 10 A.M.–8 P.M. daily mid-June–early Sept., $1 per ride or $10 for 20). The city also recently introduced a new bumper-boat ride and waterslide (mid-June–early Sept., $5 unlimited rides), and a bouncy castle (5–8 P.M. Mon.–Thurs., $5).

Rounding out the experience is the miniature aquatic petting zoo at the **Save the Bay Exploration Center** (175 Memorial Blvd., 401/324-6020, www.savebay.org, 10 A.M.–4 P.M. daily late May–early Sept., $5, free for children under 3). The educational facility is filled with tanks of local marine life, and while it's not big enough to offer an entire day's worth of activities, it makes for a fun stop on the way to or from the neighboring beach.

Daily parking for nonresidents costs $15 on weekends, $20 on holidays, and $10 on weekdays. The parking lot holds about 600 cars and fills up fast in summer. If you're staying for longer than a week, it's worth considering a nonresident parking sticker good for the entire season (Memorial Day–Labor Day) for $80.

While First Beach may be where all the action is, quite a few locals actually consider Second Beach, also known as Sachuest Beach, as the best beach for sunning in all of Newport. A short distance east on Purgatory Road and Paradise Avenue, it's a three-mile-long crescent directly facing the Atlantic and sheltered by Eastern and Sachuest Points, making it ideal both for walkers and sun bunnies. Daily parking, plenty of which is available in several lots, costs $10 on weekdays and $20 on weekends—prices that clearly reflect the beach's immense popularity; nonresidents can also buy a season parking pass for $140.

Finally, traveling down Sachuest Point Road and then bearing left will bring you to Third Beach, the least popular but no less beautiful stretch of sand that faces northeast toward the Sakonnet River, which opens to the Atlantic just south of here. The river keeps the water even warmer than most Rhode Island beaches, making this an excellent spot for a dip. The beach is also much more secluded and quiet than First or Second Beaches, making it a nice spot for quiet contemplation away from the crowds. Parking fees are the same as Second Beach—$10 on weekdays and $20 on weekends.

## OTHER BEACHES

Aquidneck Island has many other beaches, each with its own personality. The easiest to access from downtown Newport is **King Park** (Wellington Ave., 401/846-1398, free), right off Thames Street; it attracts swimmers, sunbathers, and picnickers, although it's small, and its harbor-side setting is not the most relaxing of vistas. A better view can be had just off of Ocean Drive on the edge of Newport Harbor at **Fort Adams State Park** (Harrison Ave., off Rte. 138, 401/847-2400, www.riparks.com/fortadams.htm, sunrise–sunset daily, free), which boasts 100-plus acres of manicured lawns, picnic spots, beaches, soccer fields, and boating and camping areas. Each year it's home to the area's folk and jazz festivals as well as a plenitude of private clambakes. Also on Ocean Drive, **Brenton Point State Park** has a medium-size parking area and a small pavilion with changing rooms. The beach is too rocky and rough for swimming, but it can be ideal for beachcombing and lying in the sun.

Perhaps the most intriguing beach in Newport is **Bailey's Beach,** which is really only accessible on foot, by bicycle, or by way of the Bellevue Avenue bus. In the late 19th century, Bailey's Beach became the ultraexclusive playground for Newport's wealthiest summer residents—over the years, however, enough people protested about the restricted access that city council intervened on their behalf. Much to the horror of local elitists, research into the original layout of Bellevue Avenue revealed that a good chunk of Bailey's Beach was in fact not legally private at all. A public easement was granted, finally giving the public access.

As you drive north along the eastern shore of Aquidneck Island, you'll come to a couple of other good beaches. **Sandy Point Beach** is a wide, peaceful expanse of sand along the Sakonnet River with picnic facilities, grills, and restrooms. Parking costs $10 on weekdays and $20 on weekends. **Teddy's State Beach,** near Stonebridge Marina off Point Road in the Island Park section of Portsmouth, offers a quiet crescent of pebbly sand beside the preserved section of Old Stone Bridge, with picnic tables and good spots for angling. Admission is $7 on weekdays and $10 on weekends.

## BICYCLING

Newport and the rest of Aquidneck Island are prime territory for bicycling enthusiasts. Any of the walking or driving routes described in this chapter are excellent for two-wheeling, as is all of Conanicut Island and Jamestown, especially in and around Beavertail State Park. You can rent bicycles in Newport at **Ten Speed Spokes** (18 Elm St., 401/847-5609, www.tenspeedspokes.com, 10 A.M.–6 P.M. Mon.–Fri., 10 A.M.–5 P.M. Sat., noon–5 P.M. Sun.).

## BOATING

Newport is one of North America's great sailing and yachting hubs. There are several full-service marinas in town, including **Bannister's Wharf** (off Thames St. in Newport Harbor, 401/846-4500, www.bannisterswharf.net/bann-mrna.htm), a relatively small facility in the heart of downtown Newport with gas, diesel, ice, electricity, showers, laundry, and a phone.

Look to **Adventure Watersports** (142 Long Wharf, 401/849-4820, 9 A.M.–6 P.M. daily) for rentals of personal watercraft, outboard motorboats, kayaks, sailboats, and dinghies. The company also customizes boat tours, fishing trips, and charters. At Fort Adams State Park, **Sail Newport** (60 Fort Adams Dr., 401/846-1983 or 401/849-8385, www.sailnewport.org, office 9 A.M.–5 P.M. daily year-round, dock office 8:30 A.M.–8:30 P.M. daily late May–early Sept.) rents 19–22-foot sailboats and provides professional instruction for all ages.

A great all-around resource for boat charters

of all kinds is the **Newport Yacht Charter Association** (28 Church St., 401/849-3340, www.newportcharters.com), a member-based organization of brokers who can help you choose the right vessel for you or your group to charter. These brokers work with about two dozen vessels that specialize in sailing, motor yachting, and sportfishing, and the boats vary from 155-foot schooners that can accommodate 80 passengers to 36-foot sailboats that can handle up to 15. Rates vary from $25–75 pp for a two-hour sunset sail to several thousand dollars for a weeklong charter.

Sea kayaking is a very popular activity along Newport's winding shoreline and up and down the Sakonnet River—there are hundreds of inlets and quite a few islands to explore within reasonable paddling distance of Newport and the surrounding towns. The best sources for rentals include downtown Newport's **Adventure Watersports** (142 Long Wharf, 401/849-4820, 9 A.M.–6 P.M. daily) and **Newport Kayak Company** (18 Elm St., 401/849-7404).

## FISHING

From spring through fall, Newport is one of the Eastern Seaboard's premier destinations for saltwater fishing—you'll see surf casters up and down the beaches from Newport north along the Sakonnet River and all the way around Aquidneck Island, vying for Narragansett Bay's stripers, bluefish, and bonito. Fishing from a boat in greater Newport's waters provides access to many more species, among them mahimahi, tarpon, trigger fish, Atlantic mackerel, flounder, and swordfish. There are about eight freshwater ponds on the island that are stocked with bass and trout, including Easton's Pond, which is just beyond Easton's Beach on the Newport-Middletown border.

You can rent equipment and buy bait at a number of locations, including **Zeek's Bait and Tackle** (194 North Rd., Jamestown, 401/423-1170, 9 A.M.–7 P.M. Mon.–Fri., 7 A.M.–7 P.M. Sat.–Sun.). The **Saltwater Edge Fly-Fishing Company** (561 Thames St., 401/842-0062 or 866/793-6733, www.saltwateredge.com, 10 A.M.–6 P.M. Mon.–Fri., 9 A.M.–5 P.M. Sat., 11 A.M.–4 P.M. Sun.) is your one-stop shop for information and tackle for surf casting or boat fishing in saltwater; you can also hire guides here.

There are no deep-sea fishing charters available from Newport—you'd have to head over to South County's Port of Galilee to find the nearest one.

## GAMING

If you're in the mood to take a chance, **Newport Grand** (150 Admiral Kalbfus Rd., 401/849-5000, www.newportgrand.com, 10 A.M.–1 A.M. Sun.–Thurs., 10 A.M.–2 A.M. Fri.–Sat. and holidays) is the place to try your hand at slot machines or bet on simulcast greyhound and thoroughbred racing and Florida jai alai. There's also a restaurant and bar.

## GOLF

There are a few public golf courses in the area, the most popular and dramatic being the new **Newport National Golf Club** (324 Mitchell's Lane, Middletown, 401/848-9690, www.newportnational.com, $55–150), which has quickly become one of the top destination golf courses in New England. Another good course is **Montaup Country Club** (500 Anthony Rd., Portsmouth, 401/683-0955, www.montaupcc.com, $37–47). Another option is **Green Valley** (371 Union St., Portsmouth, 401/847-9543, www.greenvalleyccofri.com, $28–68); both have 18 holes. Across Newport Bridge is **Jamestown Country Club** (245 Conanicus Ave., Jamestown, 401/423-9930, $18–19), a nine-holer.

## ICE-SKATING

At the **Born Family Skating Center** (Newport Yachting Center, 401/846-3018, www.skate-newport.com), a spacious outdoor rink on the city's waterfront, you can glide across the ice for $7 per three-hour session ($5 for seniors and children); rentals are available, as are lessons for all ability levels. A Zamboni grooms the ice hourly.

## POLO

Polo has been an important rite of Newport's summer social season since the 1880s. At the **Newport Polo Club** (Glen Farm, Rte. 138, Middletown, 6 miles north of downtown Newport between Union St. and Sandy Point Ave., 401/846-0200, www.newportinternationalpolo.com), visitors can watch matches on Saturdays June–September. These contests pit international teams from the United States and several other countries against one another. Matches start at 5 P.M. June–August and 4 P.M. in September; admission is $10. Part of the tradition is setting up "tailgate" picnics on the grounds—this is one of Newport's, and even New England's, most unusual weekly summer events.

## SCUBA DIVING

For the very reason that the waters around Newport and Aquidneck Island have proven treacherous to ship's captains for centuries, scuba divers love this part of Rhode Island. Lurking beneath the surface are countless coral reefs, ledges, and interesting—though potentially dangerous—formations, and there are plenty of sunken ships in these parts. For information on rentals, local laws and restrictions, and advice, contact **Newport Diving Center** (550 Thames St., 401/847-9293, www.newportdivingcenter.com, 10 A.M.–6 P.M. Mon.–Wed. and Fri., 9 A.M.–5 P.M. Sat., 9 A.M.–4 P.M. Sun.), which also offers charter diving excursions.

## TENNIS

The **International Tennis Hall of Fame** (194 Bellevue Ave., 401/849-3990 or 800/457-1144, www.tennisfame.org) is the only place in the United States where any two travelers can drop in and play lawn tennis. Access to the "royal" court is included with admission to the museum ($8). There are 13 grass courts open May–October.

In mid-July, the Hall of Fame hosts the **Campbell's Hall of Fame Tennis Championship** (401/849-3990, www.tennisfame.org), which draws top players from the Association of Tennis Professionals tour for the only grass-court professional tennis tourney in the nation. This is also when the Hall of Fame holds its annual induction ceremony; 2010, for instance, saw the entry of doubles stars Todd Woodbridge, Mark Woodforde, Gigi Fernández, and Natasha Zvereva, mixed doubles champion Owen Davidson, and wheelchair tennis creators Brad Parks and Derek Hardwick.

# Accommodations

Newport's summer population booms, and it's always a good idea to plan as early as possible when you're thinking of visiting. Rooms sell out especially quickly for key summer events—the folk festival, the jazz festival, the Newport Music Festival, and so on. At other times, you can almost always find a spot at one of the motels or hotels in Middletown or Portsmouth, or you can even base your operations in South County, a 20–30-minute drive from Newport over a pair of long bridges that span the Narragansett.

That being said, Newport has the greatest variety of hotel accommodations in the state, including dozens of inns and B&Bs. There are relatively few larger hotels in Newport, and those are very expensive, especially during the summer. If you're looking for mid- to low-end chain properties, try Middletown, a short drive away. Just over the Newport border along Route 138A in Middletown you'll also find a variety of ocean-side inns, motels, and hotels offering a wide range of rates. Newport proper has relatively few oceanfront accommodations, although several properties downtown overlook the harbor. If you want to be within walking distance of hotels, shops, and nightlife, downtown Newport is your best option—but keep in mind that you'll pay for this privilege.

## TIME-SHARING IN NEWPORT

One option worth considering before you decide among the many hotels and inns in the area is a luxury time-share company called **Fairfield Resorts** (800/251-8736, www.fairfieldresorts.com). It owns a number of resorts throughout the country, including four right in the city of Newport, and two more across the bay in Jamestown, the **Bay Voyage Inn** (150 Conanicus Ave., Jamestown, 401/423-2100) and **Newport Overlook** (150 Bayview Dr., Jamestown, 401/423-1886). If you're seeking seclusion and a stunning setting with great views back toward Newport, both are great picks. In Newport, **Long Wharf Resort** (115 Long Wharf, Newport, 401/847-7800) is one of the nicest luxury condo resorts in the Northeast, and its location on the harbor, just a block off Thames Street, makes it a highly sought-after destination. A smaller property nearly next door, the **Inn on Long Wharf** (5 Washington St., Newport, 401/847-7800) is also home to the very nice Long Wharf Steakhouse. **Inn on the Harbor** (359 Thames St., Newport, 401/849-6789) and **Newport Onshore** (405 Thames St., Newport, 401/849-1500) are additional options farther down Thames Street.

There are big advantages to choosing any of these six properties over a conventional hotel or inn, especially if you visit Newport often or are traveling with a family or group of friends. First, the locations and settings are top-notch. The units themselves are in large, rambling shingle buildings – in Newport they're mostly 4–5-story apartment buildings, while the Jamestown structures spread out more and feel house-like. There are studio, one-bedroom, two-bedroom, and three-bedroom properties available, and each property has a full slate of amenities, including pools, spas, exercise rooms, children's playgrounds, and the like. The units themselves are furnished with tasteful, upscale contemporary resort furniture, and all have kitchens; the majority of them have water views, depending on the property, of course. These are not historic buildings, and some critics complain they lack character. But they do make a lot of sense for the right traveler.

Fairfield Resorts is in the business of selling shares of ownership in vacation resorts, not merely renting out hotel rooms. This is something you need to keep in mind before you consider staying at one of these properties. Time-share schemes came under a lot of criticism in the 1980s and 1990s because they often proved highly inflexible or impractical, and in some cases their owners were shady at best. Fairfield Resorts is a legitimate and reputable company, but you will be hit with sales pitches if you stay at one of these properties, and that can be irksome for people uninterested in actually buying into the time-share premise.

If you simply want to vacation in one of the six condos described here, you can expect to find rates of about $150-350 per night May-October for a one-bedroom unit, up to $400-650 for a three-bedroom unit. Off-season, the rates drop by as much as 50 percent. You generally get the best deals at these places by booking via one of the major online travel websites, such as Expedia (www.expedia.com) or Orbitz (www.orbitz.com).

However, if you're willing to attend a 90-minute open-house presentation on buying a time-share condo, you can work out a very nice two-night vacation at one of the condo properties. This depends on availability, of course, and requires a reservation. If you actually buy a time-share in Newport, you're eligible to swap a week of your time there for a week at one of the other Fairfield Resorts properties in New Orleans, San Antonio, numerous cities in Florida, coastal Georgia, and South Carolina, St. Thomas (Virgin Islands), Branson (Missouri), Ocean City (Maryland), Williamsburg (Virginia), the Berkshires, Nashville, the Wisconsin Dells, Durango (Colorado), Sedona and Flagstaff (Arizona), Palm Springs, Las Vegas, and many other places. Read the terms and program descriptions carefully, and you may just find that Fairfield Resorts works for you; either way, it's worth considering as a vacation alternative.

There are a few reservations services in Newport that are useful if you're having trouble finding a room on your own. These companies can sometimes work out better rates with area inns and hotels than are available to the general public. **Bed and Breakfast Newport** (401/846-5408 or 800/800-8765, www.bbnewport.com) has more than 350 options, and there's also **Bed and Breakfast of Rhode Island** (401/849-1298 or 800/828-0000, www.visitnewport.com/bedandbreakfast).

## DOWNTOWN
## $100-150

Comfortable and centrally located, the **Chestnut Inn** (99 Third St., Newport, 401/847-6949, www.newportchestnutinn.com, $125-175) is a year-round Victorian bed-and-breakfast with several air-conditioned double rooms. The front porch makes a relaxing spot for breakfast before a day of sightseeing, boating, or touring mansions.

Once the summer home of a well-to-do Boston doctor, **The Ivy Lodge** (12 Clay St., Newport, 401/849-6865, www.ivylodge.com, $119-319) near Bellevue Avenue is a charming and refined stay at rates that can be quite good value considering the amenities offered. Dominated by a 33-foot gothic entryway, the house is filled with antiques—and many rooms come with fireplaces, DVD players, and whirlpool tubs. Daily teatime and breakfast are included, and if the savory bread pudding is on offer, don't refuse.

**The Old Beach Inn** (19 Old Beach Rd., 401/849-3479 or 888/303-5033, www.oldbeachinn.com, $135-275) is a thoroughly renovated Victorian home with exquisitely decorated rooms. A wealthy doctor built this elegant house in 1879. Guest rooms, named for garden plants and flowers, are in both the main house and a mansard-roofed carriage house that dates to the 1850s. The decor is over-the-top Victorian—the Rose Room has a lavish four-poster bed with a floral canopy, for example. Guests have use of a pantry stocked with tea- and coffee-making supplies plus snacks and bottled water. There's a gazebo out back surrounded by gardens, a brick patio, and wrought-iron patio furniture and Adirondack chairs. Continental breakfast is included. The inn is just a couple of blocks east of Bellevue Avenue at Touro Park, an easy walk to Easton's Beach.

**Attwater Villa** (22 Liberty St., 401/846-7444 or 800/392-3717, www.attwatervilla.com, $119-149), just off Bellevue Avenue, is one of the more distinctive-looking B&Bs in Newport—it was built in 1910 as a Bavarian restaurant called the Hof-Brau, which became a hoity-toity tearoom during Prohibition. The building was restored and converted into a European-style guesthouse in the 1980s. Rooms vary a great deal in size and layout, from standard units with queen-size beds to suites and apartments. The common areas are lovely, including an airy sunroom done in French country style and a very private sundeck. There's air-conditioning and a phone in every room. An expansive continental breakfast buffet is included, served in an attractive room with hunter-green walls and floral draperies.

A real gem with decent rates, considering the location near Aquidneck Park on a lovely stretch of Spring Street, is the **Samuel Durfee House** (352 Spring St., 401/847-1652 or 877/696-2374, www.samueldurfeehouse.com, $109-145), with five spacious and neatly decorated guest rooms done with mostly Federal antiques that match the home's 1803 construction; modern in-room touches include CD players, but the guest rooms do not have phones or TVs. One room has a beautiful mantel carved by Robert Adam; another has Chinese Chippendale twin beds and Asian rugs. An impressive full breakfast—a specialty is Portuguese sweet-bread French toast—is served in the stately parlor or, when weather permits, on the shaded back patio. The setting is marvelous, quiet and away from the noise of Thames Street yet an easy walk to several good restaurants.

**Inn on Bellevue** (30 Bellevue Ave., 401/848-6242 or 800/718-1446, www.innonbellevue.com, $50-135) is one of Newport's great bargains, with a terrific location and small but funky rooms with a smattering of antiques. The least expensive rooms, which are tiny and share a bath, start at just $50 on summer weekdays. Other units have whirlpool tubs. This creaky old inn is right at the upper end of Bellevue Avenue near where it meets Touro Street—you just can't find rooms this cheap in Newport in this location. As you might expect, the staff and the clientele tend to be young, outgoing, somewhat artsy, and very laid-back.

The colonial revival **Kitt Shepley House 1932** (23 Division St., 401/848-0607 or 877/362-8664, www.kittshepleyhouse.com, $99–140) is a reasonably priced 1930s B&B in the Historic Hill section of downtown. There are just two guest rooms in this cozy, easygoing inn, one of them a full suite with French provincial decor and a tile bathroom with a whirlpool tub, the other a standard room with a brass bed and hand-painted furniture.

## $150-250

The **Cliffside Inn** (2 Seaview Ave., 401/847-1811 or 800/845-1811, www.cliffsideinn.com, $170–220), not to be confused with the more conspicuous Cliff Walk Manor nearby on Memorial Boulevard, is one of the city's most distinctive inns. The Second Empire mansion was built in 1880 as the summer retreat of Maryland's governor Thomas Swann; briefly served as the campus for St. George's School at the turn of the 20th century before the Turner family of Philadelphia bought it in 1907. Daughter Beatrice Turner lived here for about 40 years, posthumously becoming one of Newport's best-known artists—her works are famous in part because they were mostly discovered only after her death in 1948, when executors of her estate found the house crammed with about 3,000 paintings, about a third of them self-portraits—alas, all but about 100 of these were destroyed by her executors. The inn has 13 guest rooms as well as three rooms in a more contemporary cottage across from the inn's front lawn and gardens. The cottage building has *three* fireplaces in each of its three suites, and there are a total of 17 fireplaces in the main mansion. Of the 100 surviving Turner works, virtually every one can be seen at this inn—some are originals and others are high-quality reproductions; you'll find them in guest rooms and common areas. The antiques that fill this property have far more character than usual hotel pieces—the Cliffside is noted for its valuable collection of Victorian beds and many other fine collectibles. The guest rooms are also notable for their elaborate and often huge bathrooms, most of which have whirlpool baths, and four even have working fireplaces—the ultimate romantic touch. Afternoon tea and quite a stunning formal breakfast complete the experience of staying at this wonderful, luxurious small hotel.

The mansard-roofed **Pilgrim House Inn** (123 Spring St., 401/846-0040 or 800/525-8373, www.pilgrimhouseinn.com, $175–255) is an informal spot along a charming stretch of upper Spring Street. This 1809 inn with gingerbread trim has 10 guest rooms with a smattering of antiques. Overall the mood is very casual and low-key; rooms have rose carpeting, and some have sleigh beds. There are no TVs or phones in the rooms; it's more a place to get a good night's sleep than to hang out. The best feature is the third-floor sundeck, which offers terrific harbor and downtown views. Continental breakfast is included.

**Inns of Newport** (401/848-5300 or 800/524-1386, www.innsofnewport.com, $210–260) is a consortium of five lavish that define luxury in Newport, and the convenient and prestigious location is a huge draw—along Spring Street, just a block from the harbor, on a quiet street just in from busy Memorial Boulevard. Dozens of restaurants and shops are within an easy stroll. At the **Wynstone** (232 Spring St.), each of the five rooms has a TV and video player, CD player, feather bed, fireplace, and two-person whirlpool tub. The decorating is exquisite and evocative of the city's Gilded Age. Museum-quality antiques fill the rooms, as do custom-made fabrics and window treatments along with elegant paintings and tapestries. The bathrooms have marble tubs and vanities, separate marble showers, terry-cloth robes, and high-quality sound systems. A full breakfast is served fireside in your guest room each morning. The similarly luxurious **Clarkeston** (28 Clarke St.) is two blocks from the water—this exquisitely preserved 1705 colonial captures the charm of early Newport, with wide-plank floorboards and vintage antiques, but the house was restored top to bottom in 1993 and now contains guest rooms with such modern touches as whirlpool tubs and air-conditioning. The sleigh and canopy beds are supremely romantic. Across the street, the 12-room **Cleveland House** (27 Clarke St.) has a Victorian ambience that's more appropriate to its late-19th-century construction. The 300-year-old **Admiral Farragut Inn** (31 Clarke St.) lives up to the elegant standards of this fine hotel group; its rooms contain Shaker-style four-poster beds and brightly painted and stenciled chests and armoires. A full breakfast is served in the authentic colonial keeping room. Lastly, the **Elm Street Inn** (36 Elm St.) is a favorite with families because several of its suites sleep four.

A stunning boutique property in the heart of downtown, the **Mill Street Inn** (75 Mill St., 401/849-9500 or 800/392-1316, www.millstreetinn.com, $145–230) occupies a 19th-century mill whose high ceilings, exposed brick walls and wood beams, and warm character have been nicely preserved. There are 23 suites, some with private decks that look out over downtown and the harbor; the upper-level townhouse suites have two floors. Continental breakfast, afternoon tea, and parking are included.

Another first-rate pick is the handsome **Adele Turner Inn** (93 Pelham St., 401/847-1811 or 800/845-1811, www.adeleturnerinn.com, $180–270). The 13 guest rooms in this stately 1855 sea captain's mansion are filled with Victorian antiques and working fireplaces along with such modern amenities as TVs with video players (there's a large selection of videos and books on loan in the library), private phones, and in some rooms, two-person whirlpool tubs. There are fabulous views of the harbor, just two blocks away, from the expansive rooftop sundeck. It's especially romantic to sit up here at night, looking down over quaint 1st Street, the nation's first gas-lighted street. Full breakfast is served buffet style; afternoon tea is also served daily.

One of the most conveniently situated small downtown properties, the **Black Duck Inn** (29 Pelham St., 401/847-4400, www.blackduckinn.com, $210–240) looks across Thames Street toward myriad shops and restaurants of Bowen's Wharf—within a 15-minute walk are countless more opportunities to browse and nosh. The inn takes its name from an infamous rum-running ship that smuggled bootleg liquor into Newport Harbor during the late 1920s. The interior is on the frilly side, with floral fabrics and wallpaper borders. Most rooms have queen-size beds, and there's a two-bedroom suite that's nice for families or friends traveling together. Some units have hot tubs.

An elaborate, almost decadent Edwardian mansion oozing with character and run by friendly innkeepers Dennis Blair and Grant Edmondson, the ◖ **Hydrangea House Inn** (16 Bellevue Ave., 401/846-4435 or 800/945-4667, www.hydrangeahouse.com, $160–229) sits near the beginning of Bellevue Avenue, just up the hill from the harbor front. The house was built in 1876, and the lavish details of that period have been colorfully preserved. Among the more enticing units among the nine spacious guest rooms and suites, the Hydrangea Suite has a king-size canopy bed, a marble bath, a double whirlpool tub with its own fireplace, Oriental rugs, a steam shower, and cable TV with a video player—it's hard to think of a good reason ever to leave your room when you're surrounded by such plush amenities. Guests are treated to afternoon tea, chocolate-chip cookies before bed, and a full breakfast that's superior to most—eggs, raspberry pancakes, and home-baked breads are among the offerings.

The enthusiastic innkeepers who run **La Farge Perry House** (24 Kay St., 401/847-2223 or 877/736-1100, www.lafargeperry.com, $210–270) have done a great job balancing a homey ambience with striking decor and furnishings. There are five spacious suites, including the John La Farge, which contains convincing reproductions of paintings by the distinguished artist and former owner, for whom the inn is named. Bathed in whites and pale blues, the Honeymoon Suite has a bathroom with a double whirlpool tub. The dining-room walls are painted with a mural of Newport from the turn of the 20th century, and deep armchairs and comfy seating fill the common areas. Depending on the season, iced tea or sherry is served during the afternoon in the formal parlor. The bright, sunny house is especially impressive when decked out with holiday decorations in December.

For an opportunity to stay in one of the Point District's most delightful waterfront homes, consider the **Sarah Kendall House** (47 Washington St., 401/846-7976 or 800/758-9578, www.sarahkendallhouse.com, $190–245), an 1871 Second Empire house with a high green turret and a porch full of comfy wicker chairs and lounges overlooking the harbor and Newport Bridge. Historic Hunter House is just a couple of doors down, and the location so near the southern end of the Point District puts many shops and eateries within a very easy stroll. The guest rooms have polished hardwood floors and four-poster beds, and are furnished with a tasteful restraint that's not always so apparent in Victorian mansions. Many units have working fireplaces. From the sitting room, lodged in the third-floor turret, terrific views are to be had of the water and Goat Island. Afternoon tea and full breakfast are provided.

## Over $250

The ne plus ultra of small luxury hotels, ( **The Chanler** (117 Memorial Blvd., 401/847-1300, www.thechanler.com, $309–1,399) feels a lot like sleeping in your own private mansion—except, of course, for the other guests. Not that you'll really notice them; you'll be too busy taking in the sumptuous decor (each room sports a different theme, from English Tudor to Martha's Vineyard), lounging in your private whirlpool tub, and gazing at the views of the ocean. Don't miss the "beach butler" service, wherein a tuxedoed staff member drives you to and from a semi-private beach and sets you up with chairs, an umbrella, a customized beach picnic, and reading materials.

A sister property of the famed Cliffside Inn, the ( **Abigail Stoneman Inn** (102 Touro St., 401/845-1811, www.abigailstonemaninn.com, $290–700) occupies a grand Renaissance-style 1866 mansion on one of the city's most prominent streets. Named for the woman who is credited with being Newport's first female entrepreneur and innkeeper, this inn—like Cliffside and the company's other property, the Adele Turner—is a slightly kooky and completely sumptuous hostelry. Among the unusual draws: original drawings by William Makepeace Thackeray, Victorian author of *Vanity Fair*; a bath menu of about 30 soaps, salts, and oils from many different nations; a pillow menu of about 20 types, from UltraFoam Deluxe to magnetic buckwheat hull to tri-down; a tea menu featuring about 45 fine blends; and a free water "pub" that features 25 kinds of bottled $H_2O$, including good old Perrier and Fiji Island artesian well water. The location is steps from Touro Synagogue and an easy walk from the harbor and Bellevue Avenue. There are just five ornate bedchambers, all with high ceilings, TVs, video players, CD players, huge whirlpool tubs or steam showers, and decor from different eras. In the Vanity Fair suite, the furnishings date to 1865–1900, while the hip Above and Beyond contains pieces dating to about 1947–1975. This guest room is truly a showstopper—a six-room, third-floor suite with a magnificent paneled library, a media center with its own fireplace, a kitchen-dining room, and many other breathtaking features. There may not be a more memorable and romantic accommodation in Rhode Island than this suite, which rents for around $650–700 per night.

**Vanderbilt Hall** (41 Mary St., 401/846-6200 or 888/VAN-HALL—888/826-4255, www.vanderbilthall.com, $340–600) was built by the Vanderbilt family in 1909 as a gift to the citizens of Newport. After being used as the Newport Men's Social Club and later as headquarters for Doris Duke's Newport Restoration Foundation, it was turned into a luxury hotel in 1997. Today it ranks among the most regal accommodations in Rhode Island, and even if you don't stay here, consider attending one of the famously decadent afternoon teas (tea is free for hotel guests). There are just 50 guest rooms, all of them decorated individually and many with unusual touches such as romantic sleeping lofts reached by spiral staircases. The Old World billiards room is a favorite spot to sip brandy and smoke a cigar, or play hearts with a few friends in the card room. There's also a clubby, white-glove restaurant open to the public—you'll want to dress nicely. There's nothing hip or trendy about this hotel, but if you want to feel like one of Newport's elite summer visitors of a century ago, Vanderbilt Hall is an excellent place to stay.

A favorite of families or groups of friends seeking luxurious harbor-side accommodations that has full kitchens and plenty of legroom, the **Newport Bay Club and Hotel** (337 Thames St., 401/849-8600, www.newportbayclub.com, $395–450) may lack the history of some of the city's colonial and Victorian inns; on the other hand, it outshines the majority of them in terms of both amenities and water views. All things considered, the rates aren't bad either, starting at $359 on summer weekends but with deep discounts for midweek stays, and staggered rates that drop to just $129 on some winter weekends. For this you get a unit that sleeps at least four (the one-bedroom suites have pull-out sofas) and as many as six, a marble bathroom with a whirlpool tub, a kitchenette with a microwave (a few have stovetops), and a nice-size living room with a dining area. Many units overlook the water, and city-side rooms have great views of the activity along Thames Street. The bi-level two-bedroom townhouses have private decks on each floor. Furnishings are contemporary and attractive, if not much more memorable than what you'd find at a typical upscale chain property. Continental breakfast is included.

One of Newport's undisputed class acts, the **Francis Malbone House** (392 Thames St., 401/846-0392 or 800/846-0392, www.malbone.com, $289–360) occupies a ravishing 1760 shipping merchant's mansion across the street from the harbor. This grand house, built by Peter Harrison (who also built the Rosewood Library and Touro Synagogue), contains 18 exquisitely furnished rooms with fine crown molding, period window treatments and fabrics, four-poster beds, Oriental rugs, and delicate colonial furniture. The walls are painted in bold colors. Many rooms have hot tubs and fireplaces. Afternoon tea and full breakfast are included in the rates. The staff is highly personable and well-trained, and yet the inn retains a surprisingly informal air. The owners also run the adjacent Benjamin Mason House, a 1750 stunner with a guest suite and guest room.

Although its name suggests a doddering old seaside hotel with rickety floors and warped-glass windows, the **Harborside Inn** (Christie's Landing, Thames St., 401/846-6600 or 800/427-9444, www.historicinnsofnewport.com, $290–350) is actually a rather new construction at Christie's Landing, smack in the heart of the city's festive waterfront. This deluxe all-suites property has spacious units with refrigerators, wet bars, sleeping lofts, and balconies. The same management company has several other inns in Newport, including the Yankee Peddler Inn on Touro Street, the Jailhouse Inn on Marlborough Street, and the Newport Gateway Hotel on West Main Road in Middletown. It's a disparate group of properties with a wide range of rates.

The **Hotel Viking** (1 Bellevue Ave., 401/847-3300 or 800/556-7126, www.hotelviking.com, $240–355) feels a little too formal for an increasingly more casual town. Nevertheless, the massive top-to-bottom restoration in 2000 greatly improved the general appearance of this hulking historic hotel, which has a neat location equidistant from Broadway's hip eateries, Bellevue Avenue's mansions, and Spring Street's antiques shops. The 237 guest rooms, while nicely maintained, are rather dull, and a kitschy early-1960s addition to the hotel spoils its overall appearance. Public areas retain the glamour of yore, but somehow the Viking's overall effect is unintentionally retro. The hotel was built in 1926 and was one of New England's premier addresses for many years—it was commissioned by the owners of Bellevue Avenue's summer "cottages" as a place to put up guests and visitors. Furnishings are reproduction Queen Anne and Chippendale, but the rooms have all the modern trappings you'd expect of a luxury full-service hotel: TVs with in-room movies, climate control, hair dryers, irons and ironing boards, and phones with data ports. There's also a pool, a health club, and a sauna as well as a lavish spa, which is perhaps the highlight of the property. The hotel's Bellevue Bar and Grille serves steaks, seafood, and other favorites. The rooftop bar is great fun, affording terrific views of downtown and the harbor—it's a fine place to meet up with friends or take a date.

The **Hyatt Regency Newport** (1 Goat Island, 401/851-1234 or 800/233-1234, www.newport.hyatt.com, $310–580) is a pricey but superbly maintained option that occupies a terrific spot on Goat Island, with outstanding views back toward downtown and of the Point District in one direction and the Newport Bridge and Jamestown in the other. The staff here is extremely well-trained and professional, and the facilities and rooms are top-notch, but make sure you're going to use all these features before you spend the money to stay here. These facilities include a full-service spa with massage, facials, and treatments, plus an exercise room, a tennis court, indoor and outdoor pools, two restaurants, and lots of meeting space—it's a popular site for conventions. If you're angling for luxury, book one of the bi-level loft suites that have private balconies overlooking the water.

The **Newport Marriott** (25 America's Cup Ave., 401/849-1000 or 888/634-4498, www.newportmarriott.com, $240–475) is a grand luxury hotel on the edge of downtown. Some rooms open onto a bright atrium and others face downtown or the harbor. It's very attractively furnished, but this is still a large (319-room) chain hotel, and it doesn't exactly ooze with character. Amenities abound, including an indoor pool, outdoor deck, and an extensive full health club with racquetball courts. There are also scads of meeting rooms; indeed, the Marriott is often packed with conventioneers.

## ELSEWHERE IN NEWPORT
### Over $250

The **Inn at Newport Beach** (Memorial Blvd., 401/846-0310 or 800/655-1778, www.innatnb.com, $300–420) is the best of the First Beach–area properties—it's just across the street from the water and sand, and the staff is polite and well trained. The guest rooms are decorated with attractive, upscale colonial-style furnishings, satiny striped wallpaper, and the usual amenities, including cable TV, phones, and air-conditioning. Rooms are generally smaller than at newer properties in town, but they're no less attractive—and the rates are fair. There are 50 units, some of them suites with elegant sitting areas and others with two bedrooms. Rates vary considerably depending on room size and availability, but even in summer—during weekdays—you can sometimes find accommodations here for as little as $109 nightly. Included in the price is a substantial continental breakfast. There's also a decent restaurant on the premises.

The extraordinarily sumptuous C **Castle Hill Inn** (590 Ocean Dr., 401/849-3800 or 888/466-1355, www.castlehillinn.com, $420–745) enjoys one of Newport's most enchanting settings, perched on a grassy promontory jutting into the ocean with outstanding views of Narragansett Bay. The small Castle Hill Lighthouse (circa 1890) warns ships from the rocks nearby. Accommodations are in the main Agassiz Mansion and three distinguished outbuildings. In the main building, the 1874 summer home of Harvard marine biologist Alexander Agassiz, there are 10 rooms, most of them quite large and all with well-chosen antiques—the sorts of pieces you might expect to find decorating one of the summer cottages along Bellevue Avenue. Typical features include bay views, CD players, custom marble whirlpool tubs, Oriental rugs, gas fireplaces, pitched ceilings, and stately beds with goose-down comforters and imported damask linens. It's easy to understand why these are some of the priciest rooms in Rhode Island, and yet the Castle Hill measures up where some other luxury properties don't. A small Gothic chalet-style building, once Agissiz's laboratory, now contains two handsome suites; about 100 yards from the mansion, down directly facing the water, are Castle Hill's eight more contemporary beach-house rooms; these lack the historic ambience of other units but are no less plush. Additionally, they contain galley kitchens, French doors opening onto water-view decks, full entertainment centers with video players, and double whirlpool cast-iron tubs. If it's seclusion by the sea rather than Old World style that you're seeking, these units make a superb choice. Lastly, just to the side of the mansion, a row of similarly contemporary harbor cottages sit on a short cliff over the water and also measure up to the rest of the property's very high standards. An interesting bit of literary history: Thornton Wilder was a frequent guest of the Agassiz family and based parts of his book *Theophilus North* here.

## MIDDLETOWN, PORTSMOUTH, AND JAMESTOWN
### $50-100

Middletown isn't so agrarian these days, but the **Country Goose** (563 Green End Ave., Middletown, 401/849-5384 or 877/254-6673, www.countrygoosebnb.com, $79–110) feels and looks as if it could be a farmhouse in the sticks, aside from its location on a slightly busy road. It's just a short way east of Agincourt, also an easy drive or even bike ride into downtown Newport or to the beaches. This striking white 1898 house with gingerbread trim sits on a large lawn with mature shade trees and colorful gardens. Guest rooms have high ceilings and contain a mix of family heirlooms and newer pieces; some rooms have shared baths.

The 155-room **Howard Johnson Inn** (351 W. Main Rd., Middletown, 401/849-2000 or 800/654-2000, www.newporthojo.com, $90–120) has an indoor pool, sauna, and hot tub, refrigerators and microwaves in some units, and tennis courts; there's an Applebee's restaurant next door. Some pets are welcome.

The **Sea Whale** (150 Aquidneck Ave., 401/846-7071 or 888/257-4096, www.seawhale.com, $65–110) looks a bit dreary from the exterior, but this 16-unit motel faces directly onto Easton's Pond (white chaise longues sit out back on the lawn overlooking the water). Rooms are basic but well kept, and those on the upper level have balconies; all of them face the pond and have cable TV, refrigerators, hair dryers, phones (with free local calls), and plenty of parking. It's a 10-minute walk to Easton's Beach, and you really can't beat the price for this location.

With among the lowest rates of any chain motel in the area, the **Travelodge Middletown** (1185 W. Main Rd., Middletown, 401/849-4700 or 800/862-2006, www.travelodge.com, $85–95), is a basic no-frills property with simple rooms—perfect if you're not going to spend much time back at the hotel.

### $100-150

Perched on Narragansett Bay, the **Bay Voyage Inn** (150 Conanicus Ave., Jamestown, 401/423-2100, www.bayvoyageinn.com, $103–191) is more resort than inn. With 32 suites (including kitchenettes and parlor areas), the Victorian-style building is also home to a pool, indoor whirlpools, a fitness center, and a recreation director to help arrange sailing, fishing, or biking excursions in the area.

The owners of the Howard Johnson also operate the excellent **Hampton Inn and Suites** (317 W. Main Rd., 401/848-6555 or 800/426-7866, www.newporthamptoninn.com, $89–129), which has consistently received awards for being one of the best-run hotels in the popular chain. The 95-room property, which opened in 2004, has an indoor pool, a fitness room, a business center, a tennis court, and free wireless Internet. The 24 suites have refrigerators, microwaves, coffeemakers, and separate living areas.

The nicely maintained **Newport Courtyard Marriott** (9 Commerce Dr., Middletown, 401/849-8000 or 888/686-5067, www.

courtyard.com, $95–110) is another reliable chain property a few miles north of downtown Newport. There are 130 rooms and 10 suites, plus an indoor-outdoor pool, a hot tub, a small gym, and a laundry room; continental breakfast is included.

**Rhea's Inn by the Sea** (42 Aquidneck Ave., Middletown, 401/849-3548, www.rheasinn.com, $89–123) occupies a three-story cedar-shake building that's just a five-minute stroll from Easton's Beach. Although it's in the style of the old beach houses of yore, Rhea's is contemporary through and through, and all the motel-style furnishings feel new. There are nine rooms with private baths, air-conditioning, cable TV, and phones—all the basics. Two of the rooms have separate living areas, and some have whirlpool tubs; there's a common area on each floor. This is a reliable, economical option, and there's a second branch of Rhea's inland on Route 114 (401/841-0808 or 800/474-1194).

The three-story, clapboard **Quality Inn & Suites Atlantic Beach Hotel** (34 Wave Ave., Middletown, 401/847-5330, www.qualityinn.com, $149–299) is an attractive hotel with an inviting warm color scheme and an appealingly beachy look. The ocean is practically across the street, and many rooms have views. Although it's technically outside of Newport, this attractive hotel is just steps from the town line, and it's extremely close to area beaches. Among the units, there are 43 minisuites with two phones, large work desks, microwaves, refrigerators, and coffeemakers, plus separate sitting areas. The staff can be a little rushed and cursory.

The **Seabreeze Inn** (147 Aquidneck Ave., Middletown, 401/849-1211 or 877/227-8400, www.theseabreezeinn.com, $145–285) is a small Mediterranean-style hotel with a small restaurant on the premises. The seven rooms have floral-upholstered bedding, marble-floor bathrooms, the usual amenities (cable TV, air-conditioning, free local calls), plus decks, some of which overlook the ocean and others Easton's Pond. A full breakfast is included. The owners also rent two apartments (a one-bedroom and a two-bedroom), as well as a three-bedroom house. It's an attractive place, not fancy, but the decor is cheerier than some of the more prosaic motels along this stretch.

# Food

For many years, until quite recently, it was difficult to find innovative cuisine in Newport. That's not to say that there weren't plenty of terrific restaurants, but fairly traditional seafood places, steak and chops houses, and natty old dining rooms serving haute continental and French cuisine were the rule. In the early 1990s, a few restaurants started experimenting with more interesting fare, and in the past few years several places serving highly creative regional American and globally influenced cooking have opened. Of course, it's still easy to get a traditional fried clam dinner or a juicy steak in Newport, but now there are also quite a few creative alternatives.

The island has the usual gamut of chain eateries, both regional and national, although few of these are found in downtown Newport. If you want IHOP, Newport Creamery, Burger King, Taco Bell, KFC, and their ilk, venture out along Route 138 just north of town to the intersection of Route 114.

Keep in mind that the vast majority of Newport's high-end formal restaurants have taverns or pubs attached that serve less-pricey food and demand much less fancy attire. Note that in the off-season, restaurants in Newport—and especially in the neighboring towns and on Block Island—greatly reduce their hours. Call ahead to check which meals are currently offered.

## NEWPORT
### Upscale

Even hard-core vegetarians have a hard time leaving Newport without craving seafood, what with shellfish and lobster shacks at almost every turn. Those who heed the call will fare quite nicely at **The Mooring** (Sayer's Wharf, 401/846-2260, www.mooringrestaurant.com, 11:30 A.M.–9 P.M. Sun.–Thurs., 11:30 A.M.–10 P.M. Fri.–Sat., $12–44), particularly if they're able to nab a table with a view of the harbor and sunset. No one's breaking the culinary sound barrier in the kitchen, but it's a great place to dig into a plate of fresh fried clams or seafood pie—or sample the impressively lengthy wine list.

The globally inspired, luxury-laden New England dishes that fly from the kitchen at **The Spiced Pear** (in the Chanler Hotel, 117 Memorial Blvd., 401/847-2244, www.spicedpear.com, 7:30–10:30 A.M. and 11:30 A.M.–2:30 P.M. daily, 6–9 P.M. Sun.–Thurs., 6–9:30 P.M. Fri.–Sat., $27–43) make such an impression that you could hear a fork drop throughout the elegant dining room as they're served. The butter-poached lobster with Israeli couscous is a must-try, and the fondue for two (with melted white chocolate and Godiva liqueur) alone is worth the hefty bill.

One of the city's definitive dress-up spots, **Le Bistro** (41 Historic Bowen's Wharf, 401/849-7778, 5–9 P.M. daily, $20–34) specializes in rich seafood, choice Angus steaks, and other rather elaborate continental grills. It has won countless culinary and wine awards, and the views of Newport Harbor make it a favorite place for special occasions. Service is superb, refined, and always impeccable.

Refined, traditional French food is served at the slightly formal and inviting **Restaurant Bouchard** (505 Thames St., 401/846-0123, www.restaurantbouchard.com, 5:30–9 P.M. Wed.–Mon., $19–29), which occupies the ground floor of a small B&B. Fine china and crystal along with deft service set the tone for such rarefied French fare as sliced tender lamb with red wine and a hint of curry sauce, roasted duck with currants, sautéed chicken breast with a creamy morel mushroom sauce, and wild mushroom ravioli with a walnut oil-balsamic vinaigrette.

The **Castle Hill Inn** (590 Ocean Ave., 401/849-3800, www.castlehillinn.com, lunch 11:30 A.M.–3 P.M., dinner 5:45–9 P.M. daily, $25–40), apart from having one of the most dramatic locations in the city, serves stellar regional American fare. A typical course is the starter of pulled-pork tamales with aged cheddar, smoked papaya salsa, and New Mexico red chili puree, followed by skillet-roasted spiced pork medallions with fried-potato wedges, braised summer greens, Gorgonzola aioli, and sweet-and-sour peach glaze. A favorite finisher is the Godiva chocolate soufflé with caramel crème anglaise, sugared berries, and biscotti. There are several dining rooms, all with large windows, and from many tables you'll enjoy a view over Narragansett Bay. After dark, when water views aren't such a draw, you might opt to dine in the main Castle Hill Room, which once served as the formal drawing room of this magnificent mansion by the sea.

Flash back to the 1950s and you'll appreciate the appeal of **La Forge Casino Restaurant** (186 Bellevue Ave., 401/847-0418, www.laforgenewport.com, 11:30 A.M.–9:30 P.M. daily, $17–29, in the pub $7–14), a supper club kind of spot known for its classic continental fare. To really live it up, order the chateaubriand for two with wine, a complete meal for about $50 that includes flame-grilled center-cut beef tenderloin carved tableside with a baked stuffed potato, stuffed tomato Florentine, fresh vegetables, and béarnaise sauce, plus a half-liter of house wine. With all the new eateries cropping up throughout the state serving trendy and sometimes bizarre fusions of this and that, it's refreshing to see a restaurant that refuses to depart from ancient (by culinary standards) traditions. This is an appropriate style of cuisine for the restaurant at the vaunted Newport Casino, one of McKim, Mead, and White's most distinguished works of architecture. The casino also has a much less formal Irish pub, where you can sample oysters Kinsale (baked in the half shell with blue cheese and potato stuffing), club sandwiches, fish-and-chips, and the like.

**Clarke Cooke House** (Bannister's Wharf, 401/849-2900, www.bannistersnewport.com/clarke_cooke_house.html, 6–9:30 P.M. Mon.–Thurs., 6–10:30 P.M. Fri.–Sun.) consists of two restaurants: The Porch ($23–30) is the more formal of the two, set high overlooking Newport Harbor; down at wharf level, the Candy Store ($9–23) is much more casual both in cuisine and style (in summer there's also a sushi bar serving a wide range of rolls and *nigiri*). Some locals have grumbled in recent years that The Porch is resting on its laurels, but the kitchen seems to have responded to these complaints and heavily revamped its menu. Today's French-inspired menu might offer pan-seared breast of squab with a roasted-corn pancake, foie gras, and black mission figs in a phyllo pastry, followed by roast rack of lamb with caramelized onions, potato-turnip gratin, and a minted tarragon glaze. Down in the Candy Store, which is open for lunch, Sunday brunch, and dinner, signature dishes include steak au poivre with a brandy-madeira brown sauce and Mediterranean fish stew, but you can also order simpler burgers, light pastas, and creative salads.

**22 Bowen's Wine Bar and Grille** (22 Bowen's Wharf, 401/841-8884, www.22bowens.com, lunch 11:30 A.M.–3:30 P.M. daily, dinner 5–10:30 P.M. Sun.–Thurs., 5–11 P.M. Fri.–Sat., $24–47) is a hot spot that offers a new take on the old seafood-and-chops theme, serving easily the best steaks in town. You can also order fresh seafood from the excellent raw bar. This is a pricey place, but the city's many young movers and shakers seem all too willing to pay for 24-ounce porterhouse steaks, grilled tuna steaks, and broiled lobster. Each entrée comes with a choice of sauce, which could include green-peppercorn mustard, Maytag blue-cheese butter, shallot-and-dill butter, horseradish cream, and several others. Additional house specialties include broiled scallops with shallots, lemon, parsley, sherry, and seasoned bread crumbs; and grilled pork tenderloin with apricot-sausage stuffing and rosemary-garlic *jus*. The dining room, with its pitched ceiling and timber beams, has rows of tall windows overlooking the harbor.

The **Newport Dinner Train** (departs from 19 America's Cup Ave., 401/841-8700 or 800/398-7427, www.newportdinnertrain.com, hours vary) presents a number of theme excursions, including wine-tasting and murder mysteries. On Saturday mornings, kids are invited for a tour on the Musical Magical Train, a 90-minute journey with sing-alongs, games, and entertainment by a musician. Dinner rides last 2.5 hours and run along 22 miles of track, looking out at Narragansett Bay most of the way. Both lunch and dinner rides are available, and the food is better than you might expect, given the logistics of preparing high-quality cuisine aboard a train. The menu is limited to just 3–4 entrée choices: Baby back ribs (which are excellent), sesame-crusted salmon, and chicken Vanderbilt (layered with spinach, sun-dried tomatoes, and provolone) are typical, and there's always a vegetarian option too. You really don't make one of these journeys for the culinary experience as much as to relax and take in the phenomenal views. Prices vary according to the theme, but a typical dinner ride runs $55–65 pp; package deals that include overnight accommodations at Middletown's Ramada Inn are also available.

## Creative but Casual

Bar culture had to begin somewhere in this country, and **The White Horse Tavern** (26 Marlborough St., 401/849-3600, www.whitehorsetavern.us, 11:30 A.M.–2:30 P.M. and 5:30–10 P.M. Mon.–Sat., noon–3 P.M. and 5:30–10 P.M. Sun., $29–48) may just be where it started. Opened in 1687 by the father of a pirate, the tavern features clapboard walls and huge ceiling beams typical of 17th-century architecture, but its menu, including grilled bruschetta and maple-glazed salmon, is surprisingly here-and-now.

Loud and jovial, the candlelit tavern area is the place to be in **The Black Pearl** (Bannisters Wharf, 401/846-5264, www.blackpearlnewport.com, lunch and dinner daily, $8–30)—the neighboring more formal dining room is notoriously overpriced for similar fare. Here's the spot to order up a bowl of the killer chowder (loaded with dill) and get your lobster fix; the 2.5-pounders come boiled and unadorned except with butter and a lemon wedge.

Equally fun though with a very different

The White Horse Tavern opened in 1687.

vibe is **Christie's** (351 Thames St., 401/846-8018, noon–11 P.M. Sun.–Thurs., 10 A.M.–11 P.M. Fri.–Sat., $12–23), a funky and trendy restaurant overlooking the harbor. A snazzy crowd piles into the whimsically decorated dining room, complete with swing seats and communal tables, for tasty lobster quesadillas, oyster sliders, juicy burgers, and all manner of specialty cocktails; the pomargarita is a perennial favorite. Later in the evening on weekends, dancing takes over the bar area, which fills with a crowd that defines casual chic.

Since new owners took over the **Canfield House** (5 Memorial Blvd., 401/847-0416, www.canfieldhousenewport.com, 5–9 P.M. Tues.–Fri. and Sun., 5–10 P.M. Sat., $16–24), the restaurant has greatly improved. It's an elegantly faded Second Empire yellow house near the Tennis Hall of Fame. The restaurant's Patio Pub is a nice spot for a drink. Try the flatiron steak with maple-peppercorn demi-glace, braised pork shank with white beans and carrot-raisin slaw, or simple stream mussels in lemon-herb broth.

Always bustling **Yesterday's and The Place** (28 Washington Sq., 401/847-0116, www.yesterdaysandtheplace.com, 11 A.M.–9 P.M. Sun.–Thurs., 11:30 A.M.–10 P.M. Fri. and Sat., dining room $22–30, pub $6–13) sounds, smells, and looks like a festive tavern—the main room is filled with revelers, has a long bar and a tile floor, and is usually noisy nearly to a fault. But off to one side you'll find a smaller wine bar and dining room called The Place that turns out pricey but first-rate globally inspired fare such as a Thai lobster "martini" with a vermicelli-noodle stir, seafood Napoleon with a coconut-lemongrass broth, and rack of lamb with a pecan-mustard crust with fennel and apples. Although the fancier part is refined, nowhere at Yesterday's will you encounter attitude or stuffiness—and plenty of folks dine in the more formal section and guzzle in the other. The food in the pub, though simple, is also commendable; try the house salad with apple, walnuts, and feta over seasonal greens, or the grilled yellowfin sandwich with wasabi mayo and sliced fresh tomatoes.

**Cafe Zelda** (528 Thames St., 401/849-4002, www.cafezelda.com, dinner 5–9 P.M. daily, $15–22) has two identities—on one side it's an informal and always packed pub; on the other side you'll find a dark, romantic, and festive space that's more appropriate for a full meal. You can order from the same menu on either side. The food has improved greatly in recent years, with specialties that include balsamic-roasted half chicken with herb gnocchi and filet mignon with port wine Gorgonzola. Either space can get loud, which makes it a pretty fun spot to hang out with friends; there's also a significant wine cellar.

A trendy yet understated seafood place on Lower Thames, **Scales and Shells Restaurant and Raw Bar** (527 Thames St., 401/846-FISH—401/846-3474, www.scalesandshells.com, 6–10 P.M. Mon.–Thurs., 6–11 P.M. Fri.–Sat., 4–10 P.M. Sun., $12–25) prepares fresh fish and shellfish in an austere yet handsome dining room—just a few mounted fish on the walls decorate this airy room with hardwood floors. The simply prepared, outstanding fish can be ordered mesquite-grilled, broiled, or with a couple of other straightforward treatments; monkfish, bluefish, and tuna are among the possibilities. Also consider the clam pizza. The lobster *fra diavolo* for two is a signature dish and a favorite.

One of Newport's true standout dining experiences, **( Asterisk** (599 Thames St., 401/841-8833, 4–10 P.M. daily, $20–31) occupies an old service station on Lower Thames—the pair of glass garage doors now act as enormous windows for the front of the dining room. Exposed air ducts, an unfinished floor, and an open kitchen create the feeling of a little food theater, where the entertainment lies as much in watching the chefs at work as it does in dining on their always delicious creations. The food is not overly complicated or stylized, just good, and the menu always offers plenty of specials. House specialties include a lobster salad starter that can easily work as a meal, rare tuna with a green peppercorn sauce, crispy duck with stir-fried rice and a ginger-lemon-soy glaze, and classic *moules et frites* (mussels steamed and served with fries, Belgian style). There's a long bar on the left where you can dine or sip cocktails or wines by the glass (the wine list is extensive). Asterisk is self-assured without being stuffy and handsome without feeling formal. The crowd is good-looking and chatty, and you'll feel at ease here whether dressed to the nines or clad in jeans and a tucked-in shirt. There's live jazz on weekend evenings.

**Puerini's Restaurant** (24 Memorial Blvd. W., 401/847-5506, www.puerinisrestaurant.com, 5–9 P.M. Mon.–Thurs., 5–10 P.M. Fri.–Sat., $13–20) is a great local spot for outstanding Italian food, with both classic and innovative preparations that use the freshest ingredients—consider homemade linguine with hot sausages and fresh tomato sauce or lasagna layered with spinach pasta, fresh veggies, and several kinds of cheese. This attractive space is a short distance from busy Thames Street. Reservations are not accepted, which can translate to a wait on weekends.

Another locals' favorite for Italian, **Sardella's** (30 Memorial Blvd. W., 401/849-6312, 5–10 P.M. Mon.–Thurs., 5–11 P.M. Fri.–Sat., 4–10 P.M. Sun., $14–18) is right next to Puerini's and favors a more southern Italian menu. Chicken marsala, eggplant parmigiana, grilled New York steak with roasted-garlic butter, pasta Bolognese, and gnocchi with sweet Italian sausage, cherry peppers, and plum tomatoes are recommended dishes. In warm weather there's dining on the patio overlooking the garden.

With a stylish young chef who describes herself as a "Gen-X Martha Stewart," the eclectic fare at **( Salvation Cafe** (140 Broadway, 401/847-2620, www.salvationcafe.com, 5–10 P.M. Sun.–Thurs., 5–11 P.M. Fri.–Sat., $7–16) verges on pan-Asian and sometimes dazzles, sometimes comforts, but always piques one's curiosity; the appetizers are especially fun. Consider the sweet-potato shrimp cakes with a coconut-lime dipping sauce, the pumpkin ravioli tossed in cinnamon sage butter and freshly shaved Asiago, or the Kama Sutra Platter of pork vindaloo, chickpea masala, cucumber *raita*, and garlic naan. Cocktails are also recommended. This is truly Newport's oddest, hippest, and happiest little bistro—an eclectic fun house that draws a hip young crowd and is decked in feather boas, a giant retro Gulf gas station sign, lime-green walls, a gilt-framed painting of a pink flamingo, and all sorts of other curiosities.

Another of Broadway's wonderfully offbeat restaurants, **Tucker's Bistro** (150 Broadway, 401/846-3449, www.tuckersbistro.com, 6–10 P.M. daily, $17–24) has a pair of narrow dining rooms with ruby-red walls, elaborate chandeliers of several shapes and sizes, gilt mirrors, and—from the tableware to the water glasses—mismatched everything. It feels like a Victorian salon; oil paintings, which are for sale, line the walls; and soft music, varying from Billie Holiday to Verdi operas, plays in the background. The decadent, flavorful food matches the ambience. You might sample orange-ancho-glazed pork chops or shepherd's pie layered with sweet corn and mashed potatoes; Thai shrimp nachos are an arresting appetizer, or knock back a stein of Newport Storm beer while noshing on steamed mussels on a cold winter evening. Homemade Bailey's is another specialty of the bar. For dessert, consider white chocolate, dried cherry, and pecan bread pudding.

One of Broadway's hottest spots for both dining and socializing is **Pop** (162 Broadway, 401/846-8456, 5 P.M.–1 A.M. daily, $5–19), a swank lounge with mod furnishings and a terrific menu of small plates and tapas. Vidalia onion and ricotta ravioli, Black Angus and lamb burgers, vanilla gelato with candied figs, and grilled salmon BLTs with yellow tomatoes are standouts. Plenty of devotees come simply for the ambience, glowing fireplace, and sophisticated cocktails.

## Pizza, Pasta, Seafood, and Pub Grub

If you're craving barbecue, head to the **Smokehouse Cafe** (at the Mooring, Sayer's Wharf, 401/848-9800, 11:30 A.M.–10 P.M. Mon.–Thurs., 11:30 A.M.–11 P.M. Fri.–Sat., noon–10 P.M. Sun., $7–22), which serves a delicious smoked Cajun catfish sandwich and another piled high with jerk calamari steak. Other specialties include St. Louis–style pork ribs, jumbo Gulf shrimp with a chili marinade, and grilled salmon with sesame-ginger sauce. The smoked corn and crab chowder is another favorite. The dining rooms overlook the harbor, and there's an expansive waterfront patio too.

**Rhode Island Quahog Co.** (220 Thames St., 401/848-2330, 11:30 A.M.–10 P.M. Sun.–Thurs., 11:30 A.M.–11 P.M. Fri.–Sat., $12–24) operates with a gimmicky theme, serving just about anything you can imagine with clams in it; if you stick to these dishes, you'll probably come away with a pretty decent meal. Portions are enormous, so you won't leave hungry. Steamers, clam cakes, chowder, baked cod, and all the usual seafood standards are offered, plus some inventive specials such as pan-seared red snapper with lobster and guava sauces. The cavernous dining room with cream walls and royal-blue napery is also the site of live music on many nights; in warm weather, grab a seat on the attractive tiled terrace overlooking the activity of Thames Street.

A favorite summer hangout of college students as well as quite a few visitors, the **Red Parrot** (348 Thames St., 401/847-3800, www.redparrotrestaurant.com, 11:30 A.M.–10 P.M. Sun.–Thurs., 11:30 A.M.–11 P.M. Fri.–Sat., $7–17) is a rambling restaurant with large open windows that face out over Thames Street and across the way to Perry Mill Market—ceiling fans whir overhead as friends fill up on booze and comfort food. Specialties include Jamaican jerk chicken, Oreo mud pie, lobster pizzas, mussels, fajitas, and big colorful frozen drinks that fall on the brash side. There's nothing especially subtle about this place, but there's no denying that it's good fun.

It looks, feels, and actually smells like one of those Old World Italian restaurants on Federal Hill in Providence, and sure enough, **Ristorante Lucia** (190B Thames St., 401/847-6355, noon–10 P.M. daily, $9–13) turns out some of the best pies you'll ever taste. This simple BYOB space, as popular for takeout as for dining in, prepares a superb white pizza with mascarpone, mozzarella, fontina, provolone, onion, and roasted sweet peppers, plus a memorable eggplant parmigiana version. The real house specialty, however, is the artery-clogging *crescentina*, a stuffed and fried pizza with Northern Italian lineage. Order it stuffed with pepperoni and provolone, or perhaps with Romano beans, a spicy tomato sauce, and herbs. There's also a wide range of pastas, salads, and Italian grills available. **Brick Alley Pub and Restaurant** (140 Thames St., 401/849-6334, 11:30 A.M.–10 P.M. Sun.–Thurs., 11:30 A.M.–10:30 P.M. Fri.–Sat., $6–16) has long been a reliable, if usually quite crowded, standby for tasty comfort fare. The long menu includes Cajun catfish, broiled chicken and artichoke sandwiches, bacon burgers, spinach fettuccine, and sole Veracruz. The staff is friendly and fun, and the crowd is lively and loud: This is not a place for a quiet evening.

## Ethnic Fare

Sushi fanatics converge on **Sumo Sushi** (198 Thames St., 401/848-2307, www.sumosushinewport.com, 11:30 A.M.–10:30 P.M. daily, $10–25) for exquisite Japanese food plus several Korean dishes and stews. Korean barbecue is one classic dish, as is spicy kimchi stew with beef, pork, vegetables, and tofu. Several Japanese teriyaki grills are also offered. From the sushi side of the menu, maki rolls include spicy scallop, salmon skin and cucumber, pickled radish, and more than a dozen others. The sedate, warmly furnished dining room is a calm alternative to some of Thames Street's busier restaurants.

For simple, hefty Mexican fare, drop by **Freaky Burrito** (16 Broadway, 401/847-7276, 11 A.M.–9:30 P.M. Mon.–Sat., 3–9:30 P.M. Sun., $4–8), a simple but attractive taqueria that serves up delicious quesadillas, burritos, and the like, all packed with both traditional Mexican and American ingredients.

## Quick Bites

The local chain **Newport Creamery** (181 Bellevue Ave., 401/846-6332; 208 W. Main Rd., Middletown, 401/846-2767, www.newportcreamery.com, hours vary, $4–8) is often compared with the larger Massachusetts-based Friendly's Ice Cream chain. It's a cheap and cheerful option for light diner-style food, including seasoned French fries, club sandwiches, turkey-and-Swiss melts, burgers, chicken fajita wraps, fried clam dinners, and an extensive selection of breakfast foods. Of course, the big draw is ice cream—there's a long dessert menu of sundaes and awful-awfuls, those thick shakes that Rhode Islanders seem completely addicted to.

Down-home **Charlie's Good Egg** (12 Broadway, 401/849-7817, 10 A.M.–4 P.M. daily, under $8) is a downright downcast diner that serves excellent breakfast food that includes about 10 kinds of pancakes such as chocolate chip, banana, and raisin. Omelets as well as several kinds of French toast are specialties, and sandwiches and pastas are served later in the day. The no-frills space is packed with old photos and mismatched furnishings that seem to have been culled from garage sales.

You might not expect one of Newport's best-kept secrets to be a restaurant at the Hyatt Regency, but ◨ **Pineapples on the Bay** (Hyatt Regency Newport, Goat Island, 401/851-1234, 11 A.M.–10 P.M. daily late May–mid-Sept., $7–13) has a terrific setting by the pool and looking out over the Newport Bridge and Narragansett Bay, a great spot at sunset. Hotel guests often eat here, of course, but not a lot of nonguests know about it. The food is fresh and interesting—mostly creative seafood, sandwiches, and the like, and dining is at teak patio tables. It's the perfect spot to sip a fruity drink and enjoy the breezes off the water.

**Taste Buds** (406 Thames St., 401/846-1577, 11 A.M.–8 P.M. Mon.–Sat., noon–6 P.M. Sun., under $5) is a simple storefront café on Thames Street offering a wide and varied selection of coffees and teas, plus Italian ices, pastries, and cookies. More substantial fare includes spicy tuna sandwiches, hummus platters, and Brie and sun-dried tomato sandwiches. There are just a few tables, but this is also a good takeout option.

## Java Joints

An elegant storefront space on Lower Thames, the **Steaming Bean** (515 Thames St., 401/849-5255) is hung with framed artwork and has a dining room of pretty blond-wood tables and chairs, plus a wide selection of magazines to peruse. It's Newport's favorite yuppie haunt for coffees and snacks.

Say what you will about the franchising of America, the **Starbucks** (212 Thames St., 401/841-5899, 5 A.M.–10 P.M. Sun.–Thurs., 5 A.M.–11 P.M. Fri.–Sat.) on Thames Street is a lovely inviting space with a particularly comfy seating loft overlooking the action down below.

With stainless steel tables, white-vinyl chairs, exposed air ducts, and a postindustrial feel, ◖ **Jack and Josie's** (111 Broadway, 401/851-6900, 10 A.M.–6 P.M. daily, $5–9) brings a touch of big-city cool to Newport's increasingly trendy Broadway area. The kitchen produces excellent lighter fare, including salmon BLTs, citrus-chicken salad, portobello and roasted red pepper paninis, great smoothies, and a wide range of teas and desserts. There's an Internet and computer station on one side of the room and free high-speed Wi-Fi throughout the place. A few discreetly placed flat-screen TVs show sporting events and videos. This is a terrific spot simply to hang out and read the paper or to grab a quick tasty meal.

## Gourmet Goods and Picnic Supplies

Here's an option that's great fun if you're staying someplace with a kitchen, dining area, or patio, or if you're planning an outing on a boat or to a nearby park or beach: **McGrath Clambakes** (401/847-7743, www.riclambake.com) delivers lavish summer meals to your location hot and ready to serve. Included in each meal is a one-pound lobster, steamed clams, corn on the cob, butter and broth, mussels, baked potatoes, and Portuguese sausages. The minimum is 10 people per meal, and 24 hours' advance reservation is required.

**Portabella** (136 Broadway, 401/847-8200, 8:30 A.M.–5 P.M. Mon.–Sat., 11 A.M.–4 P.M. Sun.) sells delicious prepared Italian foods, octopus salad, lasagna, homemade sauces, gourmet groceries, artisanal breads, and dozens of cheeses. There are plenty of tables and chairs inside as well as seasonal outdoor seating.

Another terrific source of delectable gourmet prepared foods and groceries is the **Market Newport Gourmet** (43 Memorial Blvd., 401/848-2600). A short sampling of goodies regularly available here includes white-bean salad, bay scallops wrapped in bacon, designer sandwiches, and many kinds of casseroles and grills. Chocolates, vinegars, jams, cheeses, exotic produce, and smoked meats are also sold.

Head to **Harvest Natural Foods** (1 Casino Terrace, off Bellevue Ave., 401/846-8137, 11 A.M.–8 P.M. Mon.–Sat., 9 A.M.–7 P.M. Sun.) for organic and natural groceries, deli fare, and prepared salads and soups.

## MIDDLETOWN, PORTSMOUTH, AND JAMESTOWN
### Upscale

Offering among the best views of any restaurant in the area, the **Bay Voyage Inn** (150 Conanicus Ave., Jamestown, 401/423-2100, hours vary so call ahead, $22–34) is worth the drive or ferry ride from Newport, mainly so you can sit in the elegant dining room and gaze back across Narragansett Bay toward the city. Sunday brunch is an especially popular occasion at this historic inn that's part of the ubiquitous Eastern Resorts time-share company. Creative world-beat cooking is the hallmark of the kitchen—you might start with pan-seared ostrich fillet served with a potato-and-goat-cheese galette, sample an entrée of seared monkfish sautéed with a citrus risotto, wild mushrooms, and asparagus, and finish with a dried-cranberry demi-glace. Everything on the menu is wonderfully fresh. The dress code requires a jacket.

Little Jamestown also has one of the best regional Italian restaurants around with ◖ **Trattoria Simpatico** (13 Narragansett Ave., Jamestown, 401/423-3731, noon–10 P.M. Sun.–Thurs., 9 A.M.–11 P.M. Fri.–Sat., $18–32). Among the stellar starters is a velvety lobster bisque with fresh blue crab, sweet corn, and a goat cheese crostini. Jumbo pan-seared sea scallops with a pineapple-soy miso broth, steamed black rice, and sautéed julienne vegetables shows the chef's skill with both healthful and globally inspired dishes. In fact, the Italian menu borrows heavily from the U.S. Southwest, Asia, and Latin America. Corn-crusted halibut with double-corn polenta, black bean salsa, and grilled jalapeño and tomato jam is another terrific dish. Traditionalists can still find a delicious linguine with shrimp in white wine. There's live jazz many nights, and in summer you can dine alfresco beside the lush gardens.

The **Sea Fare Inn** (3352 E. Main Rd., Rte. 138, Portsmouth, 401/683-0577, 5–10 P.M. daily, $18–32) is a bit off the beaten path from Newport, but it's worth the trip for what many consider the best seafood on Aquidneck Island. Inside this stately white 1880s house fronted by elaborate gardens and a neatly trimmed lawn, dining rooms abound with Oriental rugs, white-linen tablecloths, fine crystal, and fireplaces.

## Creative but Casual

Oyster lovers find bliss at the friendly and bare-bones **Jamestown Oyster Bar** (22 Narragansett Ave., Jamestown, 401/423-3380, 11:30 A.M.–9:30 P.M. Sun.–Thurs., 11:30 A.M.–10 P.M. Fri.–Sat., $7–18). The pub-meets-bistro ambience is the place to slurp bivalves fresh from local waters.

The **15 Point Road Restaurant** (15 Point Rd., Portsmouth, 401/683-3138, www.restaurant.com/microsite.asp?rid=336272, 5–9 P.M. Tues.–Thurs., 5–10 P.M. Fri.–Sat., 4–9 P.M. Sun., $14–22) is a dapper cottage right by the beach at Stonebridge Marina in the Island Park section of Portsmouth. Popular with northern Aquidneck Island locals and folks on the Sakonnet Peninsula, 15 Point Road is also a great option for Newporters seeking creative, deftly prepared cooking without the crowds and high prices of Thames Street. First and foremost, this handsome little dining room is a neighborhood restaurant, and the staff is easy-going and friendly, always willing to explain a particular preparation or ingredient. Seafood is a major player here—the Block Island scallops over a nest of angel-hair pasta in a light garlic–white wine sauce are terrific. The kitchen also turns out a tender and delicious beef Wellington and a rich lobster casserole baked in sherry and cream and topped with puff pastry.

## Steaks, Seafood, Pizza, and Pub Grub

A casual longtime favorite in Jamestown, **Chopmist Charlie's** (40 Narragansett Ave., Jamestown, 401/423-1020, www.chopmistcharlies.com, 11:30 A.M.–9 P.M. daily, $11–17) serves lunch and dinner, specializing in local seafood. Fairly straightforward and always fresh stuffies, calamari, shrimp steamed in beer, scampi, and seafood au gratin are doled out in generous portions.

Right on the Newport-Middletown border, **Johnny's Atlantic Beach Club** (55 Purgatory Rd., Middletown, 401/847-2750, 11 A.M.–10 P.M. daily, $14–22) is a spacious eatery whose greatest attribute is its fine views over Easton's Beach and the ocean, enjoyed from an enormous patio or a similarly large dining room. The menu presents a fairly standard variety of somewhat upscale seafood dishes, including grilled yellowfin tuna, baked scrod, and lobster salad; rack of lamb Grand Marnier is popular among the nonfish fare.

A reasonably priced and dependable option in Middletown, the **Glass Onion** (909 E. Main Rd., Rte. 138, Middletown, 401/848-5153, 10 A.M.–9 P.M. daily, $10 and up) serves a nice range of American food, much of it with oniony themes: French onion soup, onion omelets, and the ubiquitous (if dreaded) fried onion blossom. Pastas and grills round out this menu that's especially strong on seafood. The dining room is rustic and warmly decorated, with two large fireplaces, hanging greenery, and tall ceilings.

## Ethnic Fare

There's above-average sushi to be found at **Sea Shai** (747 Aquidneck Ave., Middletown, 401/849-5180; Long Wharf Mall, Newport, 401/841-0051, www.seashai.com, 11:30 A.M.–2:30 P.M. and 5–10 P.M. daily, $8–22), known for feather-light tempura, fresh sashimi, and decent Korean dishes such as classic *bulgogi* (sliced barbecue beef).

**Tricia's Tropi-Grille and Oasis Lounge** (14 Narragansett Ave., 401/423-1490, www.triciastropigrille.com, 4–9 P.M. daily, $12–18) occupies a cozy light-yellow clapboard house along Jamestown's main drag. The best spot to eat is out on the large side patio. This terrific restaurant specializes in Caribbean and Asian fare such as coconut batter-fried calamari with garlic and tomatoes, Thai curry sea scallops, and sesame-chicken peanut salad.

**Ching Tao** (268 W. Main Rd., Rte. 114, Middletown, 401/849-2112, 11:30 A.M.–9:30 P.M. Mon.–Fri., 11:30 A.M.–10:30 P.M. Sat.–Sun., $6–14) serves good if somewhat predictable Chinese food. Specialties include asparagus with pork ginger sauce, hot-and-spicy crispy tofu and seafood in a sizzling red wine sauce, and mango chicken in a white-wine reduction.

## Quick Bites

In Jamestown, bright and sunny **Slice of Heaven** (32 Narragansett Ave., Jamestown, 401/423-9866, 6 A.M.–5 P.M. Mon.–Thurs., 6 A.M.–9 P.M. Fri.–Sun., $5–9), a friendly little bakery-café, packs them in for weekend brunch and breakfast served all day—try the panini sandwiches and wraps, lemon-ginger muffins, Grand Marnier French toast stuffed with berries and fresh whipped cream, and terrific mozzarella salad. There's great people-watching from the deck out front.

A cute diner with a couple of U-shaped counters, red vinyl booths, and nautical photos on walls, **Reidy's** (3351 E. Main Rd., Portsmouth, 401/683-9802, 6 A.M.–8 P.M. Mon.–Sat., 6 A.M.–6 P.M. Sun., under $8) is a local gathering spot, especially for breakfast, served all day. The kitchen serves fairly typical diner fare plus some Greek and Portuguese specialties. Consider the excellent kale soup, veal parmigiana, tapioca pudding, clam cakes, stuffies, and homemade muffins.

## Gourmet Goods and Picnic Supplies

Foodies should not miss the **Aquidneck Growers' Market** (909 E. Main St., Middletown, 401/848-0099, 9 A.M.–1 P.M. Sat. mid-June–late Sept.), held on the grounds of the Newport Vineyards and Winery. You can find both organic and conventional produce, fruits, flowers, wine, baked goods, breads, jams and jellies, sauces, cheeses, and other delicious foods.

# Information and Services

## VISITOR INFORMATION

Pamphlets, brochures, and visitor information are available from the **Newport County Convention and Visitors Bureau** (23 America's Cup Ave., next to the bus terminal, 401/849-8098 or 800/976-5122, www.gonewport.com), which also provides packages with discounted rates on lodging and restaurants and has a switchboard for last-minute hotel availability.

The area's major hospital is **Newport Hospital** (11 Friendship St., Newport, 401/846-6400, www.lifespan.org/newport). Local pharmacies include **Rite Aid** (268 Bellevue Ave., Newport, 401/846-1631, www.riteaid.com) and **CVS** (181 Bellevue Ave, Newport, 401/846-7800, www.cvs.com). A handful of banks are found on Thames Street, and several ATMs are located on Thames Street and on Bellevue Avenue, as well as at the bus station and in convenience stores. Free **Internet access** is available in several local cafés, including **Jack and Josie's** (111 Broadway St., Newport, 401/851-6900, www.jackandjosies.com), and for guests only at the majority of hotels in town. Fax and shipping services are offered at **The UPS Store** (270 Bellevue Ave., Newport, 401/848-7600, www.theupsstore.com).

## MEDIA

Most locals read the **Providence Journal** or the **Boston Globe** as their daily news source. Newport's local newspapers are the **Newport Daily News** (www.newportdailynews.com) and **Newport This Week,** which is mainly an arts and entertainment weekly.

# Getting There and Around

## BUSES

From T. F. Green Airport, **Cozy Cab** (401/846-2500 or 800/846-1502, www.cozytrans.com) runs a shuttle-bus service to Newport; the cost is about $20 each way.

**Peter Pan Bus Lines** (401/751-8800 or 888/751-8800, www.peterpanbus.com) offers service from Boston's Logan Airport via Boston several times daily; the cost is about $60 round-trip (about $50 round-trip if you're coming from Boston rather than from the airport). The ride takes about 90 minutes, not counting the short trip from Logan to Boston's South Station. Peter Pan also makes a run from Newport to New York City, connecting through Providence; the fare is about $100 round-trip.

The **Rhode Island Transportation Authority (RIPTA)** (401/781-9400, www.ripta.com) has bus service from T. F. Green Airport to Newport, and also from Newport to Providence and to the University of Rhode Island in Kingston. Buses arrive in Newport at the station attached to the Newport Visitors Center on America's Cup Avenue, in the middle of downtown and within walking distance to many hotels and businesses.

Within Newport, RIPTA operates local bus and trolley services that run among downtown, the outlying shopping centers, the mansions on Bellevue Avenue, and Cliff Walk and Easton's Beach. The fare is $1.75 one-way, $5 for an individual day pass, or $20 for a seven-day pass. You can park at the garage adjacent to the Gateway Information Center for just $2 for the entire day if you present the cashier with a parking ticket validated by RIPTA.

If you are heading to the sites in Middletown, consider taking the **Coyote Shuttle** (401/846-7090, www.newportvineyards.com), which leaves the Gateway Visitors Center every hour on the hour during summer, heading out to Norman Bird Sanctuary, Newport Vineyards, and other attractions for a $5 round-trip charge.

## DRIVING AND PARKING

Several car-rental companies maintain offices in Newport, including **Enterprise** (70 West Main Rd., Middletown, 401/849-3939 or 800/325-8007, www.enterprise.com) and **Hertz** (400 Airport Access Rd., Middletown, 401/846-1645 or 800/654-3131, www.hertz.com).

Driving times to Newport from major cities are: from Providence, 45 minutes–1 hour; from Boston, 90 minutes–2 hours; from Cape Cod's Bourne Bridge, 1 hour–75 minutes; from Hartford, about two hours; from New York City, about three hours. Add at least 30 minutes to these times during busy periods, including most summer weekends.

Parking in Newport is not terribly difficult after Columbus Day through about Memorial Day, but the 3–4 months of summer can be a nightmare. Much of the angst, however, seems to come from locals and regulars who are so accustomed to finding ample parking in the off-season that they kick and scream when they can't find free or metered spots on the street during the warmer months. If you can stomach paying $15–20 for a parking space in summer, you won't have much trouble finding one. There are several large municipal and private garages around town, and you can park at the garage adjacent to the Gateway Information Center for just $2 for the entire day if you present the cashier with a parking ticket validated by RIPTA, the local bus and trolley company.

## TAXIS

You can definitely get by in Newport without a car, using a cab for the few longer trips that might come up, and relying on sightseeing tour buses for trips out around Ocean Drive and to various outlying attractions. Local cab companies include **Cozy Cab** (401/846-2500 or 800/846-1502, www.cozytrans.com), **Rainbow Cab** (401/849-1333), and **Orange Cab** (401/841-0030, www.newportcabs.com).

## FERRY SERVICE

**To Providence:** The high-speed **Newport-Providence Ferry** (401/453-6800, www.nefastferry.com) runs from Providence to Newport several times daily mid-May–mid-October. The fare is $7 one-way, and the trip takes just over an hour. In Providence the ferries dock at Point Street Landing, and in Newport at Perrotti Park, near Long Wharf and very close to the bus station.

**To Block Island:** This service is provided July–early September by **Interstate Navigation** (401/783-4613 or 866/783-7340, www.blockislandferry.com). Ferries leave Newport daily at 9:15 A.M. and return daily from Block Island at 4:45 P.M.; the sail time is about two hours. The one-way fare is $10.85 for adults ($15.75 round-trip, but only for same-day passage), $10.35/$14.75 for seniors, $4.90/$7.90 for children 5–11, and $3.05 each way for bicycles. The terminal is at Fort Adams State Park on Harrison Avenue; inexpensive water taxis run passengers back and forth between Fort Adams and downtown Newport.

**To Jamestown:** Even if you have a car, it's quite practical and pleasant to travel between Newport and Jamestown via the **Jamestown-Newport Ferry** (401/423-9900, www.jamestownnewportferry.com). From Jamestown, the boat leaves several times a day for Newport's Bowen's Wharf, right off Thames Street; it crosses to Goat Island, then back to Bowen's Wharf, and then returns to Jamestown, where it is based. The earliest boat leaves Jamestown at about 10 A.M., and the last one returns at about 10 P.M.

During the morning and afternoon runs, the ferry from Jamestown makes an added stop at the 16-acre wildlife refuge of Rose Island, which also includes a lighthouse and an old military outpost named Fort Hamilton. The landing fee, if you'd like to explore it, is $3 pp ($2 if you present your ferry ticket). From Rose Island, the boat continues to Fort Adams, where you're also free to get out and wander around, and then continues to Bowen's Wharf and Goat Island. Fares vary according to the itinerary but range from $5 (from Bowen's Wharf to Goat Island or Fort Adams) to $16.50 (for a round-trip cross-bay ticket).

**Around Newport and Aquidneck Island:** There are a handful of launch services, including **Conanicut Marine Service** (401/423-1556, www.jamestown-newportferry.com), **Goat Island Marina** (401/849-5655, www.newportexperience.com/GoatIslandMarina.php), and **Oldport Marine Services** (401/847-9109, www.oldportmarine.com). These leave from Newport Harbor and can be chartered to a variety of destinations, including Fort Adams and Goat Island.

## TOURS
### By Boat

**Oldport Marine Services** (Sayer's Wharf, 401/847-9109, www.oldportmarine.com) offers cruises along Narragansett Bay and through Newport Harbor on the MV *Amazing Grace*. These hour-long narrated tours ($15 adults, $12 seniors, $5 children) are offered daily mid-May–mid-October.

**Sightsailing of Newport** (32 Bowen's Wharf, 401/849-3333 or 800/709-SAIL—800/709-7245, www.sightsailing.com) gives daily narrated tours aboard sailboats of three different sizes that generally last 75–90 minutes.

**Classic Cruises of Newport** (Christie's Landing, 401/847-0298, www.cruisenewport.com) has daily cruises from Bannister's Wharf. These include the 72-foot schooner *Madeleine*, the high-speed Prohibition-era *Rumrunner II*, and the *Arabella*, a 155-foot sailing cruise yacht that makes three-night excursions out to Martha's Vineyard, Nantucket, and elsewhere in the Northeast. Fares range $18–25 pp.

Narrated tours of Newport Harbor are given aboard the *Flyer* (401/848-2100 or 800/TO-FLYER—800/863-5937, www.flyercatamaran.com), a 57-foot catamaran with a large sundeck and room for more than 65 passengers; amenities include a full cocktail bar and a shaded seating area. This is a beautiful ship and a great way to experience Newport's glorious waters. The boat departs from Newport four times daily May–October. Rates are $30 pp for most sails, $35 pp for the sunset runs.

Leaving from Bowen's Wharf, the schooner **Adirondack II** (401/847-0000, www.sail-newport.com) also makes five 1.5-hour sightseeing trips around Newport Harbor, Fort Adams, and area lighthouses each day. Rates range from $27 adults, $22 children for a morning cruise to $35 adults, $30 children for a sunset cruise. It is also available for private charters.

There are several other sailing charters in town as well. **America's Cup Charters** (401/846-9886, www.americascupcharters.com) offers daily sunset cruises aboard actual America's Cup–winning yachts. These tours sail around Narragansett Bay.

## On Foot

**Newport Historical Society Walking Tours** (401/846-0813, www.newporthistorical.org) offers extremely interesting walks through the city; these leave from the Museum of Newport History at Brick Market on Friday and Saturday May–October. The appeal of **Native Newporter** (401/662-1407, www.nativenewportertours.com) is right in the name—the owner-operated company comprises guides that reach back over three generations of Newport history. They present several forthright and factual Newport tours ($25–45) replete with an insider's knowledge of the city that can include one mansion tour. The best value, however, may be the group's special "Mansion Madness" tour ($95), which includes admission to *every* major mansion for one day of sightseeing. There's no set time limit, so the only limit to how many marble staircases and gilded chandeliers you can see is your own stamina and stomach for displays of conspicuous consumption.

Kids especially enjoy **Ghost Tours of Newport** (401/841-8600 or 866/334-4678, www.ghostsofnewport.com), which leave from the Newport Marriott. These lantern-led strolls show the dark and creepy side of the city. A newer addition are **Dead Man's Tales** (401/952-6601, www.deadmanstalesri.com), a group of costumed actors that lead "pirate tours" of Newport. Tours leave from Bowen Wharf several times during the day and once at night.

Last but not least, and not exactly on foot, the Segway tours given by **Segway of Newport** (438 Thames St., 401/619-4010, www.segwayofnewport.com) have proven to be an immensely popular way to explore the city. The only downside is that tours are a bit pricey at $75 pp for a complete circuit around Ocean Drive or a trip up Bellevue to gawk at the mansions. A better deal may be to rent one of the store's electric bicycles for $50 for up to four hours or $75 for the day; nonelectric ($15) and folding bicycles ($25) are also available.

## By Bus

**Viking Tours of Newport** (Gateway Visitors Center, 401/847-6921, www.vikingtoursnewport.com) provides narrated trolley tours of the city that include Ocean Drive and the mansions along Bellevue Avenue. A standard tour is $24 pp; package deals that include tours of one or more of the mansions are also available.

## By Train

People sometimes get confused about the sightseeing trains that depart from Newport's vintage rail depot (19 America's Cup Ave.). The **Newport Dinner Train** (401/841-8700 or 800/398-7427, www.newportdinnertrain.com) is a separately owned company from the other excursion train that uses these tracks, the **Old Colony Railroad** (401/849-0546, www.ocnrr.com). On either train you'll enjoy a breathtaking journey over tracks used for passenger service for roughly a century from the 1860s; they wend for five miles along the shore of Narragansett Bay, well beyond the Newport Naval Base, and then five miles back. The Old Colony tours are given in vintage rail cars that are about 100 years old; tours last about 80 minutes and cost $8 for adults.

## By Air

The most thrilling way to see Newport is by jumping on a birdie with **Bird's Eye View Helicopters** (401/843-TOUR—401/843-8687, www.birdseyeviewhelicopters.com), which offers surprisingly affordable trips through the sky above Aquidneck. For a different perspective on Newport's mansions, a fly-by over The Elms, The Breakers, Rosecliff, and Marble House is only $59 pp with a two-person minimum ($49 pp with three people). Other tours, including buzzing a few lighthouses, range $89–129 pp. And if you'd like to take the stick yourself, you can sign up for a half-day "Introduction to Flight" class—a private lesson in helicoptering that culminates in a flight over Newport with you at the controls.

# www.moon.com

DESTINATIONS | ACTIVITIES | BLOGS | MAPS | BOOKS

**MOON.COM** is ready to help plan your next trip! Filled with fresh trip ideas and strategies, author interviews, informative travel blogs, a detailed map library, and descriptions of all the Moon guidebooks, Moon.com is all you need to get out and explore the world—or even places in your own backyard. While at Moon.com, sign up for our monthly e-newsletter for updates on new releases, travel tips, and expert advice from our on-the-go Moon authors. As always, when you travel with Moon, expect an experience that is uncommon and truly unique.

**KEEP UP WITH MOON ON FACEBOOK AND TWITTER
JOIN THE MOON PHOTO GROUP ON FLICKR**

## MAP SYMBOLS

| | | | | | | | |
|---|---|---|---|---|---|---|---|
| | Expressway | C | Highlight | ✈ | Airfield | ⚑ | Golf Course |
| | Primary Road | ○ | City/Town | ✈ | Airport | P | Parking Area |
| | Secondary Road | ◉ | State Capital | ▲ | Mountain | ▲ | Archaeological Site |
| | Unpaved Road | ✹ | National Capital | + | Unique Natural Feature | ♦ | Church |
| | Trail | ★ | Point of Interest | | | | Gas Station |
| | Ferry | ● | Accommodation | | Waterfall | | Glacier |
| | Railroad | ▼ | Restaurant/Bar | ♠ | Park | | Mangrove |
| | Pedestrian Walkway | ■ | Other Location | ⊡ | Trailhead | | Reef |
| | Stairs | △ | Campground | ⛷ | Skiing Area | | Swamp |

## CONVERSION TABLES

°C = (°F - 32) / 1.8
°F = (°C x 1.8) + 32
1 inch = 2.54 centimeters (cm)
1 foot = 0.304 meters (m)
1 yard = 0.914 meters
1 mile = 1.6093 kilometers (km)
1 km = 0.6214 miles
1 fathom = 1.8288 m
1 chain = 20.1168 m
1 furlong = 201.168 m
1 acre = 0.4047 hectares
1 sq km = 100 hectares
1 sq mile = 2.59 square km
1 ounce = 28.35 grams
1 pound = 0.4536 kilograms
1 short ton = 0.90718 metric ton
1 short ton = 2,000 pounds
1 long ton = 1.016 metric tons
1 long ton = 2,240 pounds
1 metric ton = 1,000 kilograms
1 quart = 0.94635 liters
1 US gallon = 3.7854 liters
1 Imperial gallon = 4.5459 liters
1 nautical mile = 1.852 km

**MOON RHODE ISLAND**
Avalon Travel
a member of the Perseus Books Group
1700 Fourth Street
Berkeley, CA 94710, USA
www.moon.com

Editors: Elizabeth Hansen, Leah Gordon
Series Manager: Kathryn Ettinger
Copy Editor: Christopher Church
Graphics Coordinator: Tabitha Lahr
Production Coordinator: Tabitha Lahr
Cover Designer: Kathryn Osgood
Map Editor: Albert Angulo
Cartographer: Kat Bennett, Chris Henrick

ISBN: 978-1-59880-762-2

Text © 2012 by Michael Blanding and Alexandra Hall and Avalon Travel.
Maps © 2012 by Avalon Travel.
All rights reserved.

Some photos and illustrations are used by permission and are the property of the original copyright owners.

Front cover photo: Sunset Sailing around Newport # 049_49 © Discover Newport
Title page photo: © Stuart Monk/123rf.com

Printed in the United States

Moon Spotlight and the Moon logo are the property of Avalon Travel. All other marks and logos depicted are the property of the original owners. All rights reserved. No part of this book may be translated or reproduced in any form, except brief extracts by a reviewer for the purpose of a review, without written permission of the copyright owner.

All recommendations, including those for sights, activities, hotels, restaurants, and shops, are based on each author's individual judgment. We do not accept payment for inclusion in our travel guides, and our authors don't accept free goods or services in exchange for positive coverage.

Although every effort was made to ensure that the information was correct at the time of going to press, the author and publisher do not assume and hereby disclaim any liability to any party for any loss or damage caused by errors, omissions, or any potential travel disruption due to labor or financial difficulty, whether such errors or omissions result from negligence, accident, or any other cause.

# ABOUT THE AUTHORS

## Michael Blanding and Alexandra Hall

Michael Blanding and Alexandra Hall met working five feet from each other as editors at *Boston Magazine,* where Alex covered food and fashion, and Michael wrote about politics and crime. Since then, they've traveled the world together, dodging bicycles on the streets of Ho Chi Minh City, breaking an axle on a safari in South Africa, and closing out nightclubs in Reykjavik, Paris, and Buenos Aires (not an easy feat!). But wherever their travels have taken them, they've always loved returning to New England for its mix of natural beauty and culture.

Alex grew up on Boston's South Shore and studied at Wheaton College and Le Cordon Bleu in Paris. After several years as a senior editor for DailyCandy and editor for *Fashion Boston,* she is now back at *Boston Magazine* as executive editor for lifestyle. Michael grew up west of Boston, attended Williams College, and was a staff writer and editor at *Boston Magazine* for five years. Now a freelance magazine writer, he has also taught journalism at Emerson College, Northeastern University, and Tufts University. His first book of investigative nonfiction, *The Coke Machine: The Dirty Truth Behind the World's Favorite Soft Drink,* was recently published.

Together, Alex and Michael have written for publications including *Condé Nast Traveler, Bon Appétit, Town & Country Travel, New England Travel, Yankee, Boston Magazine, Elle Decor, Continental, Business Traveler, The Nation, The New Republic, The New York Times, The Boston Globe,* and AlterNet. They were married on the rustic shores of Maine's Moosehead Lake, where Michael wore a kilt and Alex donned red heels and white feathers. They now live in Boston's Jamaica Plain neighborhood with their cat, Catsby, and their six-year-old son Zachary and four-year-old daughter Cleo, who have fast become two of the best-traveled kids in the world.